When It's All Her Fault

One Man's Journey from a Dead to a Dynamic Marriage

First Edition

Greg A. Tilford
Janet K. Tilford, CPCC
Gene H. Benedict, MA, LPC

FigAPPLE PUBLISHING

Cover art by AROD Web Design Inc., www.arodweb.com.

Editing by Willow Literary Services, www.willowliteraryservices.com.

Publication inquiries may be directed to FigApple Publishing at www.figapplepublishing.com.

Additional information about the book can be found at www.WhenItsAllHerFault.com.

ISBN-10: 1453879242
ISBN-13: 978-1453879245

Foreword

I did not know what to expect when Greg and Janet first gave me a copy of their book, *When It's All Her Fault*. Refreshingly, they do not present themselves as experts who have mastered their relationship and everyday life. Instead, they give the reader honest and raw insights into their nearly thirty-year struggle to have a successful marriage.

I once heard someone say that telling someone to "be yourself" is the worst advice one can give. This is simply not true. Authenticity is required for all healthy relationships. Who we are determines what we do, not the other way around. Greg and Janet let you see them as they truly are, two people learning to take responsibility for themselves. The great news is, like Greg and Janet, we are all a work in progress. This is an amazing book by amazing friends. Join them on their journey and enjoy.

Dr. Randy Speed, ThD
Senior Leader, River of Glory, Plano, Texas

Dedication

This book is dedicated to every man who has fought to have a
healthy and happy home and feels like he has failed.

There is hope.

There are answers.

Contents

Acknowledgements

I know there is honor in going last, but there is Someone that I need to acknowledge first and last, and that is my friend, Lord and Savior, Jesus Christ. I believe that in Jesus lies the secret to all joy, healing and restoration. Without Him there is no life.

I am indebted to the love of my life, Janet, who has weathered many storms with me and now shares many joys. If it were not for your ability to love, and love deeply, this book would have never been written, and more importantly, we would not have the life we are enjoying now.

Hand-in-hand with Janet are my adult children, Brett and Josh. You have always been a joy and a motivation to climb higher. I love you both dearly. Maggie, you are truly a daughter-in-love. The amazing relationship you and Brett share helped spur Janet and me to seek out God's best for our marriage as well.

Next is my co-author, brother-in-law and friend, Gene Benedict. Thank you for believing in me and for being willing to share your life experience with me. You have the healing hands of Jesus.

I want to thank Paul Hegstrom who plowed the nearly impregnable ground of healing and restoration in front of me. Without your pioneering work and personal experience in the area of Arrested Emotional Development, this book would not be possible. You had the courage to ask God about the failures in your own life, to listen to His answer and to act on it. This is a rare trait indeed.

I want to thank Terry Ramsey and Scott Peterson. You never abandoned me, and your wise words helped pave the way for my healing.

I also want to thank Tommy Rocka. When I was panicked and at my lowest point, you gave me wise counsel.

To Rick and Joyce Nelson and Robert and Lori Romano, you have been friends of ours for many years and will be for many years to come. Thanks for being part of our past and our present.

To Robin Hudson and Chris Owen, you both loved and accepted me without judgment. You also loved Janet through many dark hours. Thank you.

I am indebted to Julie Cavassa for "coaching the book." Your honest critique and insights shaped this book in many ways and helped spur both Janet and me to dig a little deeper.

To Grace Prichard who tirelessly turned my convoluted prose into something that resembles the English language. I know it is your love of Janet and me, and of people in general, that motivated you to help. Thank you.

Last I dedicate this book to every man who has the courage to face his deepest fears. You are more than conquerors.

Preface

I find myself in a peculiar position today. I am writing a book that I never intended to write. This is not a book about theory. It is intensely personal. It is about my life and how it affected others that I love deeply. It has a happy ending, but it only reaches it after nearly fifty years of pain and suffering.

If you have tried to get help for your marriage from friends, pastors, marriage counselors, or virtually anyone who would listen, and you still struggle in your marriage, this book is for you. This book is man to man. Although Janet provides her insights, it is primarily about my journey. If you are a woman who wants to better understand a man in your life, you may find this book beneficial.

Although at the heart of this book is our marriage, it is not a book on marriage. You can only have a healthy marriage with two emotionally healthy people. This book is about my journey toward health. It is my prayer that this book will help set you on that journey. If you are single or already divorced, you may find answers. Every journey starts with a single step. Make the step that leads you to a healthier you, and healthy, enduring relationships will follow.

...you will know the truth, and the truth will set you free [1]

This book is about freedom.

Marital Bliss

May your fountain be blessed, and may you rejoice in the wife of your youth

- Proverbs 5:18

Dearly Beloved, we are gathered together here in the sight of God – and in the face of this company – to join together this man and this woman in holy matrimony, which is commended to be honorable among all men; and therefore – is not by any – to be entered into unadvisedly or lightly – but reverently, discreetly, advisedly and solemnly. Into this holy estate these two persons present now come to be joined....

Marriage is the union of husband and wife in heart, body and mind. It is intended for their mutual joy – and for the help and comfort given on another in prosperity and adversity. But more importantly – it is a means through which a stable and loving environment may be attained.

Those words were spoken over Janet and me over thirty years ago. Our marriage ceremony was small. The thought of having a large group of people with nothing to do but focus on us terrified me. I can still remember looking up the long aisle at the church with sweaty palms and my heart pounding so hard that it was visibly moving my tie on my chest. Although the aisle was probably no more than thirty feet long, it looked like the length of an entire football field. I walked slowly and deliberately, hoping that I would not trip over my own feet and fall flat on my face. Somehow I made it to the front, turned and looked straight down the main aisle. I tried to focus on the back of the church, so I would not notice the faces staring at me.

Everything changed when the song for the processional started, and I saw Janet walking up the aisle. She looked so beautiful! Her long hair was pulled up, and she walked with such confidence and grace. It was at that moment that everyone and everything else in the room disappeared. It was just Janet and me. All was right with the world.

When Janet and I were planning the wedding, my goal was to have the bare minimum of family present. I did not even invite either of my brothers or their families who lived out of town, so I would not trouble them with the long trip to South Carolina. "Not bothering" someone was a big theme in my extended family.

When my mother died my dad did not tell his family about her death until the last minute, so they would not have the time to travel. Using my twenty-twenty hindsight, I can see that not bothering others had more to do with not bothering and stressing my dad, but this was never spoken or questioned. It was a life commandment of our family, and life commandments were rarely questioned; they were simply lived and obeyed. I carried on the tradition. The fewer people at the wedding the better, and the fewer people that I invited, the fewer people there would be that I needed to somehow satisfy, and that was fine with me.

Still, Janet managed to sneak an invitation to a few of her friends. I felt like Janet had broken our agreement to just invite family, and I felt like she had betrayed my trust, but I did not show it or discuss it at the time. After all, this was our wedding day, and the day of our wedding was supposed to be a perfect day.

I knew that Janet had some minor flaws even before I married her. She had a fiery temper, and there was no end to her determination when she thought she was right. If one word summed her up, it was persistence. Still, I believed her strengths outweighed her weaknesses. Janet was highly intelligent, and she could converse on almost any subject, which was a trait that I highly valued.

When we were dating we spent hours at our favorite restaurant, Cerillos Pizza Boat, munching on pizza and just talking. Growing up I felt that I had to tailor my conversation to those of others because no one had the range of interests I carried. I liked cars and motorcycles, but I also liked science. My friend's read comics. I preferred *Scientific American*. I pretended to be interested in football or basketball just to have friends. But Janet was different. Her interests were as broad as mine. They were not identical, but we had enough overlap that we always found something to discuss.

Janet had another trait that we shared; she did not just talk, she gave hands and feet to her dreams. Ideas are interesting, but seeing those ideas turn into reality is where the excitement truly begins! I can still remember my best friend, John, trying to keep up with our conversation as he sat between Janet and me when we first met. His head was jumping back and forth between us like he was watching a ping pong tournament. When Janet and I talked, the conversation flowed like honey.

Janet was not only smart, but she had a beautiful smile and eyes so deep I would get lost in them, not to mention her gorgeous figure. I could not go wrong! So, on September 20th, 1979 we were married in my dad's church in Columbia, South Carolina.

After the wedding we snuck away avoiding Janet's sisters' plans for the traditional fanfare. John's Ford Fiesta, nearly identical to mine, was the designated decoy. I let Janet's sisters believe they had outwitted me by thinking they had our car. They decorated it in true wedding fashion from the wheels to the top of the antenna. When Janet and I were walking hand-in-hand to where I had hidden John's car, I whispered to Janet, "Don't say anything; it's not our car." Her sisters were giddy with their accomplishment. I can still hear her younger sister's taunt, "Thought you could outsmart us, didn't you?"

We were equally but quietly giddy with the brilliance of the plan. We took off from the wedding reception with Janet's sisters in hot pursuit. We both started laughing when we realized that they enlisted none other than John to drive them. Of course he was fully in on the plan, and when we zigged, he zagged and "somehow" lost us in traffic. I do not think her sisters have ever fully forgiven John for intentionally driving away in the opposite direction. When we returned from our honeymoon, John greeted us with a knife saying, "She has six sisters! She has six sisters!" He had to face all of them … alone …back at the church.

After zigging when they zagged, we drove to a parking garage on the campus of the University of South Carolina where I was studying Electrical Engineering, switched to our car, changed clothes, and drove off to our four-day honeymoon in Myrtle Beach, South Carolina. I knew that we were headed off to marital bliss. Janet loved me, and I loved her. We were compatible in every way. We only drove thirty miles before the honeymoon ended.

We started talking about our bright and hopeful future, and somehow the conversation disintegrated into a full-blown argument. I cannot remember a single detail about what was spoken, but I vividly remember feeling trapped. My fingers dug into the steering wheel as I tried to control my fears. Janet was fully on the offensive. She pressed her argument, and I tried to defend my point of view. The argument angrily went back and forth, Janet always on the offensive, I always on the defensive, like two swordsmen locked in a battle where one was obviously the master and the other the novice.

It felt like Janet was clearly the master, and my loss was only a matter of time. Eventually I went silent, not because I agreed with Janet, but because I believed it was the only way to end the argument. Eventually she gave up, and we drove the remainder of the trip to the hotel in relative silence. The mood was so cold and distant, that if I had a thermometer in the car, I am certain that it would have registered below freezing.

What happened to my beautiful wife who loved me and had just vowed "to love and honor" me? It sounded like she hated me. How could we be joyful and happy together one minute and verbally at each other's throats the next? I was completely confused and desperate to restore peace and harmony in our relationship, but how? What could I say to make her happy? What could I do? What was wrong with her to make her turn on me so quickly? Would her anger and hatred toward me drive her away one day? I hoped it would not. I prayed it would not. "Oh, God, please fix this!" I was all questions and no answers.

It Cannot Be Me

The drive to Myrtle Beach was a foretaste of the next twenty-nine years of our marriage. It was not easy. We had great areas of compatibility; we both loved a good conversation, adventure, travel, and our Lord, but we also had major areas of continuous conflict.

Family Relationships

Janet and I had completely different views of family relationships. For example, one Saturday early in our marriage the phone rang, and Janet answered the call. It was my dad. When I picked up the line, Janet silently hung on the phone. It was like she wanted to eavesdrop on our conversation. My dad and I waited silently for her to get off the line, and eventually she hung up. Later she pointed out how strangely we treated her. Strange? What was strange about wanting privacy during a phone conversation? I had no idea what she was talking about. But in Janet's big family everyone hung on the phone to chat.

The tension only grew when, after visiting with my dad, Janet asked, "How is he doing?" My dad was always doing great, and this time was no exception. He was the most positive, on-track person that I ever knew. I did not know what to say. My dad and I talked about how his nursing home business was doing and other work-related things. But we never spent much time on how Dad was doing.

Janet often said, "You do not even know each other personally." Of course we knew each other. We just did not dwell on the "touchy-feely" elements of the relationship like Janet did with her family. There were much more interesting things to discuss. Somehow Janet disapproved, and I sensed her disapproval. The dread of yet another conflict washed over me. I always was wrong in Janet's eyes. Why did the way my dad and I relate to each other have to be "wrong"? Why could it not just be "different"?

Handling Conflict

Janet was always upset over something. One day as we were driving, she became angry and her volume continued to increase until it was just shy of yelling. I hated to have arguments in the car. I always felt trapped and every one of my senses went on high-alert. My neck muscles tightened, and I gripped the steering wheel with an iron grip, but I tried to stay calm and keep everything under control. I was the level-headed one in the family. It was my job to keep our family from spinning out of control. As the argument wore on, her tone became nastier toward me. There was no pause between my response and her next retort. She pronounced every syllable perfectly and with the exact emphasis needed to make her point. She did not want to listen to reason. She was only interested in being right. It was time to lay down the law, or I believed the arguments were only going to continue to escalate and destroy our family.

I told her, "We are not going to do this."

"We are not going to do what?" she asked.

I was stunned. Where had she been during the last thousand times we argued? "This," I said, meaning these high-volume, tension-filled arguments.

Janet replied, "This is just a healthy discussion; this is no argument!"

No argument? What planet was she from? I thought she was nuts, and told her, "My parents never did this, and we aren't going to either." In all my years growing up at home, I never saw or heard my parents argue. Never. If they had a disagreement, they worked it out behind closed doors, and at a low enough volume that it did not reach the ears of anyone else in the house.

Janet said, "That is ridiculous! Everyone disagrees! You just never had any siblings to humiliate you or rough you up. Grow up!"

Now I knew she was out of her mind. Her family disagreed more than they agreed. It was not healthy, and I could not and would not live that way. I was going to stop the pattern before it became the norm for our family.

The problem was that the more I tried to control her, the more uncontrollable she became. I hated any kind of disagreement. Most conflicts are unnecessary, I reasoned. I was a peacemaker. Confrontation was as normal as breathing to Janet. To me, it was something to be avoided and only engaged in as a last resort. The very last resort.

False Accusations

Another theme of our marriage was when Janet falsely accused me of saying and doing things that just simply were not true. It was highly offensive! I was known for having impeccable integrity. At work, I was the "go-to" person who could be counted on for straight-up discussions. I did not keep hidden agendas or use manipulation. If I said something was blue, it was because I genuinely believed it was blue. If I was wrong, I was honestly mistaken. I freely admitted my mistake, and I did whatever was needed to correct the error. No one ever questioned my integrity or character.

It was not unusual in the course of one of our many arguments for Janet to pause (I assumed for dramatic effect) and say, "I have never seen a person with such integrity lie so easily."

Me, lie? Here we go again. Why not say, "I don't remember it that way" or "Are you sure?" Instead she jumped straight from a disagreement about some fact to the accusation that I was willfully lying, as if I had some innate need to be right.

If the argument continued to progress, she changed her tactic from attack to one of hurt, and she would say things like, "It is awful to watch you do anything to keep from being wrong." She genuinely appeared to be wounded. I never understood how she could go from acting like a predator to a wounded puppy, as if my being right or wrong affected her in some profound way. Her accusations of lying hurt me to the core. I always did my best to tell the truth. In most instances she would press her argument until I started to cry like a little child. I felt completely humiliated. Instead of this drawing out her compassion, she acted like she despised my tears. When I was at my most vulnerable point, I felt rejected and discarded like a piece of garbage.

Janet also loved to accuse me of being a bully. I remember bullies from the playground years. They were the ones who sought out the weaker kids and derived their enjoyment from other's fear, pain and suffering that they themselves willfully inflicted. I considered bullies to be the most despicable of all human beings. Growing up, I was the skinny kid, so I got to experience my share of being bullied. Me, a bully? Never! I went out of my way to be kind to Janet. I sacrificed my time, my wants and my desires to help her become all she could be. If anything, I was a pushover, not a bully. People told me that I was too giving to Janet. A bully? That was one accusation I never entertained. Yet, her words still wounded me. She seemed to come up with things just to hurt me. Why…I never understood.

After a long enough period of accusations, I would seek an outside perspective from someone who knew us both well. I knew there was always the possibility that I was wrong. I never received a confirmation. Each time that others confirmed my perceptions or point of view, my spirits lifted a little as I transitioned from the accused to the vindicated. But I was also saddened. Why did Janet need to say all of these awful things about me? Why did she need to be right? More importantly, why did she say things that she knew hurt me?

Once the same issue came up again, I would tell her how people agreed with me. This almost always set her off. "Who are 'these people' who agree with you?" she would ask. I almost never told her their names because they often were our closest friends, and I did not want her holding a grudge or feeling uncomfortable around them. I hoped that she would see that she was the one being difficult and was wrong. But she never did.

Even with the barrage of false accusations that Janet slung my way, I did my best to build her up, not tear her down. I told her how amazing, funny, creative, and inspiring she was. Every word was true. She told me how awful I was. She accused me of parading around as a successful man of strong character outside of the home and as a small and desperate child at home. There was no end to her insults.

Children

It did not take long after we were married for me to feel completely overwhelmed. I expected my home to be a place of refuge from the storms of life. Instead, the storms raged the strongest inside of our home.

When we were married about a year, our life started to hit a rhythm that laid a good foundation for the future. Janet was paying our bills with her job at the Veterans Hospital, and my weekend work was taking care of my college tuition. Still, we were long on month but short on money, so I joined the Air Guard to help make ends meet and to serve my country. My plate was very full, but I felt satisfied with life.

It was about this time that Janet began to talk about her dreams of having a family. It was strange that this was the one major topic that we never discussed before we were married. I enjoyed children, but I could not imagine adding to the stress level that I was experiencing with a new marriage and life in general. They were enough! I did not know the first thing about raising children. What do you do when they cry? They cannot tell you what is wrong. I did not even know how to change a diaper! The thought of the level of responsibility needed to care for a life that was totally dependent on me terrified me. I was completely unprepared and inadequate to be a father.

I told Janet, "No way! I do not want kids." Janet was shocked. She always assumed that we would have children. She even joked and said that she wanted to outdo her mother and have enough kids to field a baseball team; at least I thought she was joking.

Four years later, after babysitting our niece several times, I started to warm to the idea of having a baby. I found that I was more prepared than I originally believed. Janet was relieved! She told me that she would never bring a child into this world unwanted by his dad. It took about ten months of "practice" before Janet became pregnant. It was just before I graduated with my engineering degree from the University of South Carolina. It was perfect timing!

Around Christmas I landed a job that took us to Dallas, Texas. Our first son, Brett, was born a few months before our fifth wedding anniversary. We were elated! But the pressures felt insurmountable. There never seemed to be any money left at the end of the month, Janet really disliked me and the fighting continued. Still, Brett was a joy and we finally had something that we both agreed on; we wanted to raise our son to love his Lord and life. That was a rally call that I could answer.

Soon after attending a church in Plano, we made new friends and lived our version of the American dream. People knew that we were not having the easiest of times, but we did not appear to be living the hardest life either. We kept our fighting to ourselves. It was just part of life after all, and we chose to look on the bright side of things.

When Janet pressed me for a second child, I gave in, thinking it would take her months to get pregnant, like the first time. I wanted to have time to emotionally prepare. When she immediately became pregnant, I was overwhelmed, feeling incapable of having one child much less two. I had recently transitioned onto a project at work that was months behind schedule, and I was one of the engineers sent in to "rescue" the project that was doomed to failure if it continued the way it was going. Since it was a government project, there was no leeway; it had to be completed on time and on budget, so I put in the hours necessary to make it a success. A twelve to eighteen-hour workday was not unusual. Janet complained that I did not want to have anything to do with the pregnancy. The truth was that I was feeling overwhelmed by life. This was not my idea of how it was supposed to happen. I went into survival mode. I came home to eat and sleep, and I spent the weekends getting recharged enough to start the grind all over again on the following Monday morning.

One of my favorite activities during this time was to take Brett to a computer swap meet that was held in downtown Dallas the first weekend of every month. Brett loved to ride in the car, and I would strap him in his car seat and off we would go. We had a backpack carrier for Brett that allowed him to see over the top of my head, and we spent hours just walking around. Money was tight as always, so it was rare that I bought anything. Brett always slept on the way home, and I enjoyed the peace of the short trip back to our house.

With only one child in our lives, apartment living was adequate. However, with another baby on the way, Janet believed we needed more space to raise two growing boys. We bought a house and moved next door to the "Joneses." Work pressed on and so did life.

Janet was upset during the whole project, and she continued to accuse me of not caring about our new son, Josh. Once again things just were not what they appeared to be. Survival mode meant that I concentrated on only those things that were absolutely necessary. This meant remembering to eat, drink, breathe and work, so everyone would have a place to sleep and food on the table. The family got whatever was left of which, admittedly, was not very much. Unfortunately, I was also short-tempered. When I was tired my fuse grew shorter in direct proportion to my level of fatigue, which was substantial. I always felt remorseful when I lost my temper. Once I cooled down I apologized to the family and tried to move on. Janet never seemed to understand the pressure that I lived under. Instead of taking things off my plate, she always seemed to want to add one more thing on. Also, the feelings of complete parental inadequacy were overwhelming, so I tried to leave the parenting to Janet, who knew what she was doing much more than I.

I still did not have any idea how to raise our boys. Janet, with all her flaws, was an excellent mother. I did my best to be a study of her, but I always felt a step behind. I was lost in the world of their needs. Just remembering to feed them was an accomplishment for me! Loving and enjoying my sons was never a problem, but at times I felt like I was growing up right along with them. I had never had a normal childhood. The accolades from my dad were centered on how mature and grown up I acted. Raising our sons gave me the opportunity to see and experience life through their eyes, through the eyes of a child. It was wonderful!

Of course, this came with a price. Janet's favorite insults were, "You act like a seven year old" or "You act like a three year old!" It was both insulting and ridiculous; I was a man and not a child. I definitely did not like being compared to a three year old.

Janet appeared to enjoy being hurtful. Her words affected me like poison, and I knew that we would never make it for the long haul if her hatred toward me continued to grow. I took her jabs and insults until I reached the boiling point and all of my pent-up anger and resentment came pouring out. I never physically hit her, but I said just about anything necessary to make the argument end and restore the peace. If that meant agreeing with her position, I agreed. All I wanted was peace.

There were times our arguments went endlessly in circles. She accused me of being unable to track the conversation, when she was the one losing her way. Often it was impossible to carry on a rational conversation with her.

At times just the sound of her voice irritated me. It did not matter what she was saying...it was how she said it. I hated the way that she spoke to me. It sounded more like a parent speaking to a child than an adult speaking to another adult, but I needed her, and I knew she needed me. I was making a great salary, and I always remained faithful. I rarely even spent money on myself. I did not want to bother anyone or put anyone out. My family was my priority.

So, for the next twenty years I did what it took to keep a roof over our heads and food on the table. I steadily moved up in my job, loving the creative energy that I used in the engineering field. I felt gratified at work and very successful. But, the minute I came home, I could not do anything right. Janet was not a nag, but I always felt the pressure to do and be more than I was capable of. I still remember telling her, "If you were married to Jesus Christ, Himself, you would complain that he traveled too much!" Her expectations of me were a bottomless pit.

Celebrations

Each year, the months of August and September were by far the hardest months for our marriage. It was the time of vacations, both of our birthdays and our anniversary. This meant additional financial pressure. The money for the gifts and trips had to come from somewhere. Also, I hated both my birthday and our anniversary. I could not find anything to celebrate in either one. I did not consider my birth anything for which to throw a party. Life was such a struggle. I could celebrate surviving another year, and that was about it. I could not imagine anyone wanting to celebrate me.

Our anniversary was similar; what was there to celebrate? Our marriage was a train wreck. When I told Janet I loved her, it was genuine and true, but celebrate our marriage? It felt like celebrating a lie. If we could just make it to October, I knew that we would be fine.

It was the same theme year after year. That was the way things were, and that was the way they would always be. I spoke the words "till death do us part," and I meant them. I often wished death would come to one of us, and I always felt guilty when I wished it were Janet, so I turned the wish toward me. At least the pain would end. I did not have even a hint of suicidal tendencies. If I died it would be by God's hand, and that was fine with me.

Counseling

In our seventh year of marriage, we went for our first session of marriage counseling. Neither of us opened up much. I really hoped that the counselor would help Janet overcome her anger and hatred issues toward me. I did my best to stay in control, and Janet bit her tongue constantly to keep from unloading about me. I knew that she wanted to. I knew that Janet was just eaten up with hate for me. No one could ever imagine why, least of all me.

The counselor asked to meet alone with me once and said she understood how difficult it was for me to be married to Janet. I really felt heard by her. Then she met alone with Janet who got upset because she felt that the counselor had taken sides with me. She told Janet to read a short story about a woman who would allow her husband to physically beat her and never say, "No more!" Janet was just feisty enough to think, if anyone laid a hand on her, she would be the first one out the door.

We did not get very far into the counseling; it just made things worse. We did learn how to fight "fairly." Our counselor taught us to "never say never" and "never say always." Of course, Janet had to question how we would never say always if we were not allowed to say never (I have to admit, that even in the midst of our turmoil I always enjoyed Janet's sense of humor). We became very proficient at reminding each other of things we were not allowed to say. Basically, we sounded like a couple of children. "You are not supposed to say that; you know we agreed not to say that…" I was especially good at keeping us on the high road. I believed that if we could just forgive and move on, avoid all these discussions, maybe skip talking about the conflicts altogether, we would make it until death parted us. Then at least one of us could go on in bliss. Which one did not matter. I just wanted peace, in life or in death.

In our twenty-fifth year of marriage, just after our last child went to college, Janet said that she wanted me to leave. I was shocked. An emotional numbness swept over me, and I calmly asked her why. She simply said, "There is no reason to keep saying it; you will never change."

Keep saying what? I will never change what? When will she see it is her that needs to change? I knew everyone agreed with me. They all saw how Janet treated me.

I went to our pastor and asked him for suggestions. His first reaction was that he laughed at me. We had everything going for us. We were living a blessed life. To the outsider we had it all, two amazing, full-grown children, a wonderful house, and the quiet years every parent dreams of ahead of us. What was our problem?

He thought that I should ask Janet just what was bothering her, and he suggested a marriage counselor that others were using in the church. I came home and begged Janet to tell me what she was seeing in me and to go to counseling one more time. I knew her litany of minor complaints by heart, but I had no idea what was bothering her so much that she wanted me to leave. I even agreed to let her just tell the counselor about me. We would not even discuss her issues because I did not have any complaints that warranted a divorce. I knew marriage took hard work. Janet always wanted more than I could offer. She was the unhappy one. I would set the example, go first, and then perhaps Janet would open up and get the help that she needed.

Janet told me, "We have done me for twenty-five years." We both knew exactly how she failed constantly. I told the counselor that if he came after her first, she would bolt out the door, and I was not exaggerating.

"Please come after me first," I said. Of course I kept this between the counselor and me.

As we began our first session, the counselor asked Janet if there was any hope of saving this marriage. She told him that she had invested tons of energy into our twenty-five-year marriage, raised two sons, and that she was not going to give up, if I would consider changing. She told him all about her personal development, years of pouring her heart out to God and others, all the hours she had put into Bible studies and how far she had come. I agreed, silently noting that there was still plenty of room for her to grow and change. But I was willing to wait and get to her later.

True to his word, the counselor came after me first. I felt like a zebra being pursued by a lion. Every question he asked was targeted at exposing something negative about me. I can remember thinking, *Well, he is only doing what I asked him to do!* We were less than ten minutes into our session before he found something that I was doing wrong that cracked the shell of my nearly perfect record. I honestly was shocked but willing to listen. He told me that I was "parenting" Janet and speaking down to her. That seemed reasonable. I was definitely tired of her false accusations and unrealistic expectations of me. With all that she was doing to me, it was no surprise that some negativity had crept into my attitude toward Janet. He was right. I was clearly wrong, so I embraced what he was saying and tried to clean up my act.

Finally, in my mind, it was Janet's turn. She had absolutely no interest in pursuing anything about her. I quickly learned that if it was not all about me, it was not to be. After several months the counseling ended with me saying, "Okay, we'll try it your (Janet's) way." I took on my part, but I knew since I was not the real problem in the relationship, this was no permanent fix. Janet would be satisfied for a while, but then the cycle of her dissatisfaction would start all over again.

What do you do when the major problems of the marriage have absolutely nothing to do with you? What do you do when it's all her fault? There did not appear to be any answers. Like a man stranded in the middle of the ocean, I did the only thing I knew to do. I treaded the waters of life, enjoying the good times and enduring the bad, but never really going anywhere.

We worked at our relationship constantly. The only thing that kept me in the marriage was commitment. I had committed before God and man "until death do us part," and I intended to keep my part of the bargain. I was a man of commitment. I was a man of integrity. And deep down inside I knew that if Janet ever left me I would die.

Year Twenty-Nine

October is my favorite time of year in Texas. The oppressive heat of summer is withdrawing, and it is usually a happy time for our family, but not this year. After twenty-nine hard years, things were worse than usual in our marriage. I had not seen Janet in almost a month although we were living under the same roof. She left early in the morning and often did not come home until after I had gone to bed at night. She was making huge changes. She was losing weight. Now, nothing ever seemed to ruffle her feathers. When we had a conflict, she never became upset. She simply said her peace and walked away. She said she was "breaking cycles" that had been present in her life for years. She said that she had to minimize her time with me because "I was not safe" and "she was not strong enough yet," whatever that meant. I had never hit Janet in any way, or even been aggressive toward her, so I was not sure what this "safe" thing was about. If anything, she was the aggressor, and I was the victim.

If it had been any woman other than Janet, I would have suspected an affair. But this was Janet, and it would be going completely against her character to be putting on such a charade. Still, I was growing increasingly defensive and fearful. I verbally lashed out at the simplest of things because I was always on edge. I reacted as if she were attacking me when all she was doing was stating the facts. The less she reacted the more obvious it became that I was the one creating the problems this time. If this was not an affair, what was it, and when would things get back to normal?

I just thought Janet was going through some kind of phase, and like all phases there is a rocky period before the real breakthroughs come. *This too shall pass*, I would say to myself. I knew I had not done anything to cause her behavior. I tried to keep smiling and let her know that I loved her.

Strangely, during this same month I had my own major breakthrough where God revealed to me how my life was driven in many places by fear. I thought Janet would be ecstatic. But instead of having a positive effect, it drove us further apart.

As time passed our arguments became more frequent as I felt more threatened by the changes Janet was making in her life. After one major argument, Janet asked me to leave. She said that she had consulted with some "professionals," and they told her that as I started to work through my "issues" I could become violent.

This was totally preposterous! The most violent that I had become in nearly thirty years of marriage was when I slammed down a bowl of cereal in our kitchen a number of years before. I believed she was saying one thing, but that I was being manipulated for some other means. What that could be, I was not sure.

Janet wanted me to write a note stating that I agreed to leave if a professional said that she might not be safe as I processed through my issues. This really angered me, and at first I refused. Finally, I wrote the note clearly stating that I did not see any reason to leave, and I headed for a shower. As I went down the hall, I heard Janet say that she would have an answer from a professional by the time I finished. That fast? It felt like a complete set-up.

As I came out, I heard her on the phone. She had called a domestic violence hotline number for the county. I was in a lose-lose situation. If I stayed, she could say that I did not care about her safety. If I left it would justify her fears. I ultimately complied for her peace of mind and because I could not stand the emotional tension. I found it hard to take a breath, and it felt like someone was literally ripping me in half. I hurriedly packed a bag and left, cursing Janet all the way to my truck. What the hell did she think she was doing? What gave her the right to destroy me and our lives this way?

As I was leaving Janet assured me that this was not headed toward divorce. It was just time away to get some healing. I held onto those words like a man hanging off a cliff, holding on to the only branch in sight. There was one thing we both agreed on; our marriage was dead. Whatever our future held it could look nothing like the past.

I checked into a Motel 6 for the night. I was hurt and angry. How could the woman that I had loved for nearly thirty years, the one I had cared for, sacrificed for, treat me in such a way? Maybe it was an affair. I was devastated. My whole life seemed to be coming to an end. I felt like a puppet with Janet holding my emotional strings. If she wanted me happy, she could ask me to come home. If she wanted me unhappy, she could keep up her game forever. What would tomorrow bring? Would it be better or worse? What would I tell our children? How much should I tell them? I did not know.

I called Janet later that night and tried to talk to her, but the conversation ended badly. At this point she cut off all communication. She refused to answer my calls, phone texts or emails. I still did not think this had much to do with me. I was sure she just needed time to work things through. I continued to cling to her words, "This is not divorce."

I was spent. I turned off the light and tried to go to sleep. About this time a couple next door decided to start having noisy sex half the night. I remember thinking, *This is just great! I've just been kicked out of my own home, and I get to listen to this!* I pressed the pillow over my head and tried to sleep. Eventually, exhaustion overtook me, and I drifted into a fitful sleep.

The next day I wrote the following entry in my journal.

> *My conclusions: I don't think that this has much to do with me. I don't think Janet likes herself very much (her never-ending self-improvement). She definitely does not like men in general.*

I made an appointment for some help with our marriage counselor at the time. Why would the love of my life treat me this way? I was a kind and patient husband. I did not physically abuse her. I did not try to control her spending or vacations or any of the other things that I saw other husbands do with their wives. I was clearly the good guy, and Janet was the villain.

Then it happened. Three days later there was a knock on the door. I was greeted by a woman holding a plain manila envelope. I did not have a clue what was about to happen. I had moved into an extended stay hotel to save us money, and I just thought that it was the paperwork that I needed to sign for the lease. I was wrong. Janet had filed for divorce. The blood drained from my face. With a calmness of a condemned prisoner, I took the papers, asked a few questions, thanked her and sent her on her way. As I approached my desk, my knees buckled and I sat down and cried. She had lied. Janet had filed for divorce. Our family would never be the same. There was no turning back. It looked like a carefully planned and executed operation carried out with military precision. My marriage was over. There was one surprise. I did not die.

My journal from this time states:

Good morning daddy [that's the intimate name I use for God the Father]. [I'm] up at 4:30 a.m. again. [It] seems like I cannot get more than 5 hours of sleep no matter what I do. Well, You knew in eternity past that Janet would file for divorce. I was "served" my papers Wednesday. I've been through denial, anger, self-pity, pity of Janet, etc.... At least for now I have landed on acceptance. I am still very open to reconciliation. I know my heart matches yours in this area. But I believe this divorce is something Janet has wanted for many, many years. She just did not want to be the one to do it. It had to be my fault somehow. You know we have not had one of those marriages that just flowed, that just worked. We have both had to work very, very hard to keep it going. I guess Janet has just run out of "want to," whereas I have not. But it takes two to make a marriage. I am accepting of her position. We are both flesh and blood.

I believed every word that I wrote. Something strange happened when Janet filed for divorce. It caused a major shift in my perspective. Instead of trying to save the marriage, for the first time in my life, I truly began to look at myself.

"Things are not always what they seem" is a well-worn, but often true cliché. I believed that I was married to a truly amazing, but equally flawed woman who was the source of my pain and suffering. I believed that God would one day look at me and say, "Well done, my good and faithful servant. You loved a difficult woman. Come enter into your reward." I could not have been more wrong. As the weeks and months passed, I learned how I was more than just a major contributor to the problems in our marriage. I was the source of most of them.

Janet's Story

In November of 1978, I was apartment hunting. I came upon a house that was divided into two separate apartments near the University of South Carolina in downtown Columbia. My friend John and his best friend were also looking for a place to rent, so I mentioned the house to him. Since it was not the safest of neighborhoods, I thought that it would be great to have John, a weight lifter and sports enthusiast, as a neighbor. I leased the apartment in the back half of the house and they leased the front half.

I had one semester to complete before graduation in June, and they were freshmen at the university. We decided to move in on January first. John offered for him and Greg to help me move my things. They showed up around eight a.m., and I was immediately impressed by Greg. He took charge and was very motivated and organized. Years later I learned that he had been out until three a.m. celebrating New Year's Eve and just wanted to get finished.

I took them out to lunch as a thank you, and Greg and I talked non-stop. He seemed like a very mature nineteen year old. He was kind and patient and very articulate. What was not to like about Greg Tilford? He was very charming. Not only was I impressed but definitely a little smitten, too.

A few days later the guys moved in. We enjoyed long conversations from day one, dragging John out to the pizzeria around the corner every chance we had. Greg was in a relationship, but John said that it was ending. I decided that it was only a matter of time before Greg was free to ask me out. In the meantime, we could at least be friends.

As I got to know Greg, I discovered that he had been an entrepreneur since he was fifteen years old, employing other high school friends to install security systems he custom designed. He also worked in maintenance at his dad's nursing home in Ridgeway, South Carolina. I was impressed that he could fix anything, from taking care of the pool and septic system to designing an alarm system that would alert staff if any residents left the facility. He spoke with such compassion about the patients that he had grown up around, telling favorite stories and laughing about their shenanigans.

In April, Greg began to share his interest in God. He felt that God was somehow "out there." He asked, "Can anyone really know for sure that God exists?"

I challenged him with the question, "What if you could know?"

Greg seemed curious, so I gave him some information that explained Jesus dying on the cross to give us the relationship with God that Adam and Eve had enjoyed in the Garden of Eden. Greg later told me that he felt like his prayers were finally being heard, and he was excited to be in a relationship with God. Though we never prayed together, we now could talk about this shared belief in God. I enjoyed Greg immensely and knew that I wanted to marry him. We could talk about anything. From politics to religion our conversations were intensely challenging, in a good way.

One night my girlfriends, along with my sister Winnie and I, dressed up for a night on the town. Greg and his girlfriend were leaving the house just as I came out looking hot in my short dress and four-inch heels. Greg nearly wrecked the car staring at me. "Is that Janet?" he stuttered. In five months he had never seen me dressed up. His girlfriend was furious with his reaction, and they broke up a few days later. She had been suspicious of me all along, but I knew I had kept things at friendship only.

A few weeks later, one month before my graduation, we left "just friends" behind. Over the next five months we only went on one official date, but we spent all our free time together. It was just the two of us now, and I was in love. Our weekends were spent waterskiing at John's family lake house. In late June, we drove to South Florida to spend a few days with my sister, Peggy. We spent hours talking and swimming at the beach.

Later in July, Greg announced his plans to visit his brothers and their families in Indiana and Texas. I missed him terribly, really disappointed that there was no word from him for weeks. No love notes, post cards or calls. I busied myself, focusing on my new job.

Shortly after his return we began to discuss marriage in the fall. We had no time off from work or school for a honeymoon and very little money, so we decided to get married on a Thursday evening and go to Myrtle Beach for three nights and days.

Later that week, during an intense discussion and in a moment of extreme transparency, Greg began to speak of himself with such severe anger and disregard that I was shocked. I thought to myself, *No one could survive these thoughts. If I felt this badly about myself, I would commit suicide for sure.* Through my two years of service in the Army during the Vietnam War, I had met many struggling soldiers; however, no one with so much going for himself had ever sounded this sick.

My heart broke for Greg. His opinion of himself was in total opposition to the man that I knew him to be. Here was Greg Tilford, the man that I loved and thought I knew, revealing a dark shadow of himself. I begged him to think differently, but he would not budge.

With alarms going off all around me, I decided to look away, completely ignoring the voice in my head telling me to run. Whether it was denial or ignorance or both, I re-boarded the "love boat" and set the throttle for full speed ahead. Everyone needs someone to believe in them. I would be that person for Greg.

We began to plan our wedding. Greg was pressing for a quick visit to a Justice of the Peace. Having a Justice of the Peace marry us felt like taking the oath going into the Army. No sentiment, no emotions, no memories with my family, just satisfying some law. That meant absolutely nothing to me.

I asked if Greg would agree to a small, intimate church wedding with family only. He said yes, but he did not want us to put any burden on his family members, saying, "They would not have the vacation time, and they weren't that involved in my life really." Later when they were told of our wedding, they were deeply hurt not to have been invited. Though they were older than Greg, they considered themselves to be a closely-knit family.

When Greg realized I had twenty-five family members and this was not going to be only five or six people, I saw him flinch. But he had agreed to have them in attendance. I thought it meant that he loved me and understood the desires of my heart.

Soon after we were married, Greg and I decided to join a network marketing business with my sister Carolyn and her husband Gene. Greg was excited about the all-natural, biodegradable products. We made our plans to present the products to friends and family, and on Saturday we drove to the Tilford nursing home for me to type up a letter introducing our business.

Greg left me to work and joined his dad in his dad's office. An hour later, they came out and Greg announced, "I am going to start up a digital watch repair business. Dad will loan us the seed money for my training and a house, and I'll put the business in one of the bedrooms."

My heart skipped at least one beat. We had "our" plans. We had already invested in a start-up business. I had just spent an hour typing an introductory letter, and now I felt completely abandoned. "Our" idea felt small. I was trumped by "his dad." Greg assured me that there would be room for storing "my products," too. My products? What happened to our business? Suddenly I was deserted, holding products "we" were not going to sell. Greg's dad found a house out in the country with two neighbors in sight. They agreed that it would be perfect. Since his dad was partnering with Greg in their business and putting up the seed money, I wasn't part of the decision. Not only was our first business history, I felt betrayed and manipulated. With a seven thousand dollar loan hanging over our heads and a house forty-five minutes from my job and on the opposite side of town from where my family lived, we were far from anything I needed. I sat in silence. My stomach knotted up as I shoved down the concern and trusted that Greg would be able to provide a good income with this move.

Greg trained in Boston and learned the watch repair business quickly. I continued to work at the VA Hospital. Three months later, Greg asked me to attend a conference for watchmakers with him in Charleston, SC. I agreed to go along. On the drive home, I got curious, asking Greg why he had attended the conference. Defensively he asked me, "Why do you think I attended?"

Innocently I said, "I thought that it was to network and let the watchmakers know that you are available to fix the digital watches." Since I had not seen him introduce himself to anyone, I thought that I had missed the purpose of the trip.

Greg was furious with me. He accused me of being cold and hard. Aggressively, he began to belittle me for even considering that he should have done more at the conference. I was completely stunned. Suddenly he yelled out, "I am shy!"

"What?" I thought, *you are kidding me*. He had never acted shy around anyone. For me, shy looked like someone who could not talk. Greg was anything but that. He always appeared confident, especially in public. That the confident Greg I knew could not sell himself, was absolutely a shock. To add to my befuddled mind, he was furious at having to admit it to me.

Prior to the conference he appeared strong and confident, the leader of the pack. Now, I saw him scared, defensive, and angry. He was so uncomfortable with being less than perfect; he lashed out at me verbally, annihilating me. He was willing to say anything to keep the attention off him and on to me. Meanwhile, I saw his lost opportunity and thought to myself, *how will he ever get any watches to repair?*

Six months and seven thousand dollars of debt later, Greg discovered that it was cheaper to replace digital watches than to repair them. The business folded. We had no way to cover the debt to his dad and pay Greg's college tuition, so Greg entered the South Carolina Air National Guard. He went to Biloxi, Mississippi for seven months of basic and communication training, leaving me to live alone in a rural area of South Carolina far removed from family, friends and my job.

Before he left, I begged Greg to come back to me a man, not so fragile and self-centered. Raised as an only child, Greg was the center of his world. He had never had siblings knocking off his rough edges. After two years of marriage, I was seeing the value of siblings more and more. Annoying as siblings are, we help shape each other into well-rounded human beings. I hoped the military would help him grow up and help him think of others' needs more than his own. I also thought Greg needed men in his life to bump into for a change. I was tired of being the sibling/parent. I hoped time being treated like a man by men would grow him up. I believed that if they could just throw the right switch, he would be fine.

Isolated and on the opposite side of town from my work, family, and friends, I began experiencing sleeplessness. My dreams were about someone breaking into the house. Most nights I would lie for hours, half asleep and half awake. Sometimes there would be noisy animals outside making sounds that I had never heard. At work, I began to lose my confidence, making stupid mistakes. During lunch breaks, I found myself experiencing panic attacks around awkwardly shy people. If the conversation did not flow easily, I would start to get really nervous and sometimes end up choking on food. I would leave the table to pull myself together. I did not know what was going on.

Life began to feel like a slow death. I was unable to find my rhythm and get my feet under me. The person that needed to live isolated, away from family and without friends, Greg, was not here.

Alone, I realized that during the two and a half years of our marriage none of my needs had been considered. To make matters worse, I did not know what my needs were. Raised in the middle of a big family, I had rarely been asked what I needed or what I wanted. My desire to grow up and away from that life had landed me back to square one. I was living in another's world. Choosing what was good for me was a foreign concept. I kept waiting for someone else to choose well for me, to love me. Who would truly love me?

With Greg gone, my dad asked me if the marriage was over. I said, "No," but wondered why he had asked. Was he noticing something? We didn't discuss it further.

Sitting down to write Greg in basic training, I found myself with nothing to say. Angry and crying out in confusion, I never wrote him once. Everything in me just wanted to scream, "Grow up!"

A pattern was being established... each solution came up with its own set of problems. Surviving became a way of life. There was no such thing as thriving... just surviving. I fought the good fight, kept the secrets, and tried to become a better person.

I always believed we could beat this thing. I believed that eventually we would find the magic button. But, truthfully, I did not know what it was. For example, one day Greg was working on bandaging a bad cut, laying an old band aid used side up on the bedcover. Wanting to be helpful and thinking that he might be running low on band aids, I said, "Are you going to reuse that one?"

Instead of yes or no, Greg said emphatically, "I am not doing anything wrong." I tried to explain myself, but he interrupted me. Greg insisted, "I have a plan... I know exactly what I'm doing."

This was getting out of control. I told him, "Greg, stop. Slow down."

"You don't need to come after me. You don't know what I'm doing. If I wanted to do it differently, I would. I am smart enough to figure this out. I don't insinuate that you are inadequate. Why do you have so little confidence in me? I am an adult. I can do this."

I was taken back. I stammered, "But I was only trying to say..."

"If you only knew how you sounded!"

Caught off guard, I stumbled for words, "I know you are capable. I was just..."

"Just get away from me!" Greg yelled. "You can't just offer to help me like a normal human being."

"That's what I was trying to do. But you got so defensive so fast. I was not attacking you. I'm not worried about you messing up the bed!" I said.

"This is why people don't like you. You take something so small and blow it all up. It doesn't matter that the band aid is on the bed. It isn't hurting anything. Nothing! Can I make it any clearer for you? When someone is hurting, they don't want to be attacked. Once again you are implying that I'm a little boy. That is ridiculous!"

By this time we were both standing. I was frustrated and feeling stupid. This had been a common theme for Greg to hear me differently than what or how I had spoken. Other times, if he made a mistake or misspoke, he would lie rather than be wrong, acting just like a seven year old with his hand in the cookie jar. "I didn't do it..." or "I didn't say it..." It was horrible to watch.

By the sixth month of marriage, I had learned that whatever was wrong, "It" was unbearable, unbelievable and unfathomable. Leaving him was not an option for me because I knew that he would just go out and charm another woman, sweeping her off her feet as he had done to me. I chose to save all the women of the world from him, and I told him so. I thought I was strong enough to take it.

I stood up for myself constantly, fighting to be heard. I would not just take his lying or belittling comments. I defended myself and stood my ground. I stood for my voice and at times even stood for his. I would say, "You are Greg Tilford! You are a man of integrity. You are a strong man. You are better than this." But no matter what I did, I could not love him enough nor hate him enough to affect "It." I could not fix "It." Nothing was going to affect "It."

More than anything else, the constant strife and tension affected my health. Fifteen years later, my mental clarity disappeared, and I got so bad that I could not remember simple words like toothbrush or comb. I could not remember that I was driving. I would get three sentences into a paragraph and forget where I was going with my point. My sleep was completely disrupted by disturbing dreams. I would suddenly awaken and leave our bedroom because I believed I was in bed with the wrong man. I had dreams where I was in the middle of an unwinnable mind game, circular and dreadful, hour by hour, playing a game and always losing. I found myself praying all night that God would deliver me from what I knew as "It."

Perfection was "Its" driving force. "It" would come out falsely accusing. "It" controlled our whole world and manipulated me to everything his way. My needs were never considered by "It." Greg's most common posture was defense. If he believed he had been belittled, he would come out swinging with accusations and bullying. "It" won arguments using the power of words. For example, if I quoted him, every word had to be exact. Either it was all right or completely wrong. Sometimes it was as ridiculous as the sky is partly sunny or partly cloudy, different words only saying the same thing. "It" ran us, but I still did not know what "It" was.

There was never any intimacy with Greg. Sex was a goal, a performance always measured and usually ending with the words, "I'm sorry." It all felt horrible. I wanted to be held closely and with confidence, not by a robotic, driven, goal-oriented perfectionist.

Around our fifteenth anniversary I was diagnosed with Chronic Fatigue and Fibromyalgia. My sleep pattern became completely destroyed. I would take a nap for forty-five minutes every three hours. Most nights I only managed to sleep three hours straight through, from one o'clock to four o'clock. I suffered with asthma, arthritis, allergies, chronic pain, acid reflux, nervous stomach, and stressed out adrenals and thyroid.

Occasionally, I considered abandoning the marriage, but I did not think any of my family would believe that I was a victim of abuse.

I did not think they would be able to see someone like me, who was strong and capable, as a victim of family violence. There was no hitting. "It" was a violence of a different kind. "It" was mental and emotional violence.

After telling Greg that I could not take "It" anymore, we attended traditional counseling. The counselor caught Greg in action for the first time in twenty-five years. No one had ever seen through Greg. He always came off looking good. Greg cleaned up his behavior for six months. Without the defensiveness and false accusations, I could actually breathe easier. Our home felt safer, and with a decrease in stress I no longer felt like a constant loser. I did not need to tiptoe around him as much anymore.

When "It[1]" reappeared, I pointed out that if Greg could stop "It" for six months, he could stop "It" forever. He then held "It" away for another year. When "It" returned, "It" came back with a vengeance, ten times worse than ever, more empowered and entitled. I did not stand a chance.

From then on there was no more restraint on Greg. He would not give an inch. He began to be more accusatory and more insulting. He sought the opinions of those who would agree with him and used those opinions to hurt me. He evaded responsibility by belittling me and more arguments went nowhere. We ended up fighting over words, Greg requiring me to say the right word, not anything less than the best word. I had to pick which word was absolutely the most accurate word, with him challenging every choice, until finally I could not remember what any of it had to do

---

[1] We gave Greg's behavior the name "It" because it seemed to defy explanation. "It" was an irrational need to be right at any cost, a need to be perfect. "It" had a seemingly insatiable neediness. "It" needed me desperately. "It" needed "its" way. "It" needed to live in "its" comfort zone. "It" was like a child. "It" needed control. Unfortunately we did not get this level of clarity for many more years.

with the discussion anyway. Round and round he would go. Circular like a tornado, vacuuming me up, spinning me around and around, and then spitting me out until I would find myself completely upside down in a topsy-turvy world.

In our twenty-eighth year of marriage, I hired a Business Coach that promised to speak only the truth to me. She agreed to never say things just to build me up. If she said something about me, I promised myself that I would believe it. She promised not to lie or negatively motivate me.

At the end of each session, she would acknowledge something about me. She would say that she believed I was very courageous, brave, strong, honest with myself, powerful, a fighter, kind, loving, sensitive, wise, or willing to face my stuff. These were things that she believed she had observed during our conversation.

These were very hard for me to hear because few had acknowledged them in me except from a negative position; for instance, saying, "You are so strong or powerful...you scare me." Sometimes, she would say things that Greg also said, about me being courageous or bold or wise, but when Greg spoke them "It" would show up and bring out the great takeaway, and so I never really got to be that great trait. In the end, he would wrap it up in the negative, too. He often told me something great and then would blast me with, "You won't even accept yourself as great!"

But with my coach, it was different. Because of our agreement, I began to embrace what she was saying about me. I embraced my strengths like never before. I did my best to be my best and to believe the best about me. God had been my strength for years; we had made it through a lot together. I found a new freedom to take responsibility for my choices and began a process of choosing consciously, with more awareness. I noticed that life for me was like being a flea on the end of a dog's tail. I had been wagged here and there for years. I decided that I was not going to settle for the life of a flea, just hanging on for dear life. It was one thing to be flung around. It was another thing to cling to the one flinging me. I owned the consequences of the choices in my life and embraced the freedom to choose wisely. I grew stronger, with more focus and purpose. I wanted to be free from the abuse. I was not going to be denied.

Fifteen months later, Greg's behavior was worsening. I realized that he was encouraging me to drop any friend that was not up to his standards. This resulted in more and more isolation. His false accusations increased, and my voice was a constant irritant. His comments about me not knowing how I sounded were a broken record. Over and over he said it. It felt like being thrown to the wolves, their teeth ripping me apart, shredding me into pieces, all with the tune of "I love you deeply" playing in the background. My stomach ached, tightening up with every word, my guts wanting to just break out from the stranglehold. Each breath that I took made my stomach hurt worse. My heart was being denied the love that I so desperately wanted. "It" controlled everything, and now I couldn't even breathe deeply. How long could I continue to endure? I didn't know.

Greg would say that he cared too much to see me hurting. He wanted me happy and satisfied. His words would fall to the ground like marbles falling out of his head. We were both losing our marbles. Who would crack first?

His needs sexually were insatiable. I decided to just give more. I gave and gave. The more I gave the more he wanted. There was no satiating him. There was no end in sight. I could never do enough. Failure was always there.

However, I no longer believed him completely. I began to separate myself from his beliefs of me. I no longer saw his behavior as being something that I should love him through. His self-hatred and "mommy" issues were his, and there was nothing that I could do or say to help him solve them. I was not his mother.

That year we started our summer vacation in the mountains of North Carolina. Our hotel was cozy, with a rushing creek just outside our window. It was a great backdrop for a deep, peaceful sleep. We cycled on the Blue Ridge Parkway one day and shopped for souvenirs in the nearby towns. Greg was happy and easy to be with. After three wonderful days, we headed to South Carolina. I was driving and really looking forward to seeing my family. Greg began to fume. He looked like someone who had not eaten and was having a blood sugar crash. I suggested food and sleep, anything to help him recover before arriving in Columbia.

The further we got from the mountains, the worse Greg got. He cried that he was so tired and wanted to be with me only, no one else. I felt the isolation squeeze coming on. My options were: to give him what he most wanted, thus isolating me from my family yet again or to endure his anger and self-centeredness while somehow continuing on with the family reunion. After speaking soothing words, he verbally lashed out at me. Finally, I suggested he just stay in the back room at my sister Grace's house for the week. No need to be put out by a family reunion. I suggested he just sleep and read the week away. That seemed to calm him down.

Once we arrived at my sister's house, Greg refused to come out of our bedroom and join the family. He had had another incident of an emotional shutdown about three years before and giving him a few days away with me, meeting his every need, had helped him pull out of it then. I hoped that leaving him alone would do the trick this time.

This was the first time that Greg had shown any weak side publicly. For a week, he chose to stay in the back bedroom, saying he was emotionally exhausted. As I went out to have fun, Greg lay miserably in the back bedroom, believing he was too weak to come out and be with family. He refused to talk to anyone or see anyone for most of the week.

On our trip home, I instigated all kinds of fun and play. We went to an Atlanta Braves game and stayed over for a few days in Biloxi on the beach. We went to Ship Island and got to swim near a pod of wild dolphins. We played all the way home. He had energy as long as no one else was around. I felt smothered and controlled by his behavior. I did not only want to be with him. I loved my family and enjoyed my time with them. I wanted to have friends and lots of them. This isolated life with only Greg was horrible.

As the days went by, I began to see the set-ups, the lying, the false accusations, my sorrow over the smothering, and feelings of being strangled that I carried. I noticed that I never took deep breaths. I felt a constriction around my heart, and my chest felt very heavy. Seeing his desperation, grieved me to the core of my being. I was also realizing more and more that it had nothing to do with me.

I began to notice that against the onslaught I could not carry myself in a strong place for very long. I constantly second-guessed myself.

Early in September, we headed north on a thirty-mile bike ride. We had completed a one hundred-kilometer ride (sixty-four miles) with a group of riders one week before. This ride was hillier but half the distance. I was nursing soreness in my knees, so Greg led more than usual. With seven miles to go, I gave up the lead, tucking in behind Greg to ride in his slipstream. Since it is customary to slow down a little for the former leader to recover, Greg settled into a slower pace than we had been riding. A minute or two later, I felt recovered and shouted into the wind, "It is okay for you to pick up the pace a little."

Greg responded, "My speed is fine."

Unaware that he was struggling in the wind, I said, "I can go faster."

Greg began to lash out, cursing and yelling, "You don't know what it takes to lead. I'm doing the majority of the work. You're getting to rest!"

"No, I was saying that I'm feeling better," I replied. Trying to calm him down, pleading with him and denying that I had said anything to elicit this response, I continued, "It's just a misunderstanding."

He sent me more expletives and the overused phrase, "You don't know how you sound. Just get away from me! Leave me alone!"

At this point I was spent! It was all I needed to hear. I just wanted to escape. And that is what I did, as fast as a gunshot, I rode off. With seven miles back to the house, I needed the energy that I had left to get me home, not fight a battle out in the middle of nowhere. I put as much distance as I could between us, not wanting any more of his anger. Once I was over the next hill, I settled in doing my best to get home before I fell apart. I was emotionally drained. Riding twenty-three miles had taken a toll on me physically. My adrenaline rush during the argument left me feeling drained, leaving me with very little reserve to complete the ride. I just needed to get home.

The next day I told my friend what had happened. She was appalled! I tried to play it down, but she said, "No, you will never ride alone with him again!"

I sat shocked, playing the whole scene over in my mind. Was this as bad as she was seeing it? It had felt horrible, and I was scared the whole time riding back home, alone on a deserted road. But the fear of being alone was less than the fear of being with Greg and completely hitting the bottom with no energy left. With his reactions getting more and more out of control, I realized I was going to have to make an important decision. I didn't want to think about it, but I had to. Grief and fear came over me in waves. Was this what it looked like to come to the utter end of myself? Talking did not change things, apologizing did not change things, twenty-nine years of pleading, explaining and cajoling had accomplished the complete opposite effect of what I desired. He was getting worse than ever. There was no restraint left in him. He would say whatever he needed to say to hurt me. I did not know why. But at this point, I just needed to take care of me. My decisions from then on were based on the safety demo just before planes take off...put the oxygen mask on you first before assisting others. I had to think of myself for a change.

My eyes were opening. I did not know what to do with it all, but I was starting to acknowledge bits and pieces of "Its" effects on me. How upside down "It" was. I was hurt to the core of my being. I had given all I had to get us this far. I had raised the kids, and now I was coming to the end of myself. Greg was projecting onto me what he believed about himself all these years. He always believed that he was inadequate. He also believed that I believed that he was inadequate. I always saw him as extremely adequate and quite capable, especially at work. He saw himself little and helpless and believed that I saw him that way, too. There was no convincing him otherwise. I was done.

Greg always believed that he would be abandoned one day. He wanted to be abandoned, so he could be right. He was a victim. He would always be a victim in his mind. In the end I told him that he was getting what he wanted.

He was in control. He always was in control. I told him that every time he believed things were out of his control, he should know that he was controlling it all. I told him that he had always controlled everything. From false accusations to circular arguments, everything was in his control. My last words to him were, "No matter what happens, just know, you are in control. You have always been in control. All of this reflects your beliefs. I am giving you your way. You finally get what you always wanted." What he had not expected was my accusation of mental and emotional abuse. For me to claim fear of him was a total shock. If I could put up with it for twenty-nine years, what would make him think that I would ever really say, "No More"?

Soon after leaving the house, he began to cycle through the lashing out in anger, using our children or others against me, and then the gifting. Throughout our marriage, he had been completing the cycle every few weeks. Then it had escalated to every few days. Now, he was cycling through all three in a ten-hour period. This had been a pattern for years, but I never knew of its significance.

Needing to know more, I made a call to my brother-in-law, Gene, a family/marriage counselor and psychologist. We talked for three hours, and I described all of "It." He agreed that if what I was saying was true, Greg had the same core problem that batterers have, only with passive-aggressive tendencies.

Gene is an expert in the field of misogyny and has worked with batterers for over twenty years. He had trained us to recognize arrested development in batterers, but we never connected the dots of Greg's problems to be the same thing. Once Gene said it was misogyny, I knew what I needed to do. I had helped many women identify when it was time to leave and seek safety from a physically abusive husband. I knew the ties needed to be broken. I knew I could not send a mixed signal. Going, staying, going, staying...? I knew of the potential for the misogynist to completely lose control of himself. Since I had seen Greg's immense anger toward himself, and knew that he would feel very vulnerable at being exposed, I decided for my safety and the safety of my family to bring the marriage to an end. I filed for divorce.

Who's Right?

Clearly, one of us was wrong. Our perspectives were too different. I believed that I was a kind and patient husband who was a victim to Janet's anger and resentment. Janet saw me as a manipulative, lying, and desperate man with the emotional maturity of a seven year old and yet, incredibly capable to perform at work and in public.

The coming months provided answers, but they were not the answers that I was expecting. I found myself isolated but not alone. I had friends who loved me through the most difficult time of my life. I discovered the depth of the love of one amazing Friend in particular. It all started with sleepless nights.

The First Breakthrough

In retrospect, I can see how God set the stage for my openness even before Janet filed for divorce. Janet had asked me for many years why I was successful at work but a relative failure as a husband and leader in our home. There were definitely times that she spoke those words in complete frustration, yet her question was legitimate. She wanted the same "amazing" man at home that she saw operate in the workplace, and I was not the same person. It confused her as much as it confused me. In my mind the major difference between work and home was Janet, so the reason must be her. It could not have anything to do with me!

I was not actively searching for an answer, but God knew that I needed one. One Sunday afternoon before the separation came, He gave me an insight. It was one of those Holy Spirit moments when an unrelated thought breaks in that I knew was not from me. Janet and I had another major blow up. I was pacing around the game room while trying to sort it all through. Although I did not know it at the time, and although she had not physically left me, Janet was emotionally withdrawing more than ever before. I was angry with her. In my mind she was just rocking the boat and inviting the waves of life to come crashing in and sink our relationship. I was finding fault after fault with her words, her tone of voice, her body language, the way she approached the conflict. You name it, Janet was at fault.

Right in the middle of my blame marathon, God broke in, "At work you operate in great faith; at home you operate in great fear."

For a moment I was dumbstruck. I physically stopped moving, and I stood dead still. I thought, *Where did that come from? Certainly not from me!* In a flash all of the pieces started coming together. I realized that at work I expected solutions to problems, no matter how impossible the situation. At home I expected to fail. I quickly moved into defensiveness and fear any time that Janet and I had any kind of disagreement. I feared even the potential of conflict with Janet and would try to avoid it at all cost. I was fearful in sex that I would not be able to satisfy Janet. I was fearful of trying to be even a little "sexy" for Janet because I was afraid of failing. I was afraid to be undressed around other men in the locker room at the gym because I was afraid of being viewed as physically inadequate. I was fearful of investing money because I was afraid I might lose it. I always focused on not letting my marriage fail because I was afraid it would. I was full of fear!

I remembered a principle that I had learned in golf; you hit what you aim for. When I am hitting over water, a sure-fire way *not* to succeed is to concentrate on the water. If I say to myself, *whatever you do, do not hit the ball in the water*, nine out of ten times I will! However, if I focus on the green, I have a much better chance of hitting my real goal. By focusing on the water, it becomes my goal, and plunk, the ball will sink below the surface nearly every time.

I was doing the same thing to my marriage and family. Over and over I said to myself:

Do not get into an argument!

Do not "fail" in sex!

Do not lose any money!

Do not let others see you as you really are!

Do not, do not, do not!

My fears were driving me to a life of focusing on the *"don'ts"* and not the *"do's."* God reminded me of scriptures like, *"Perfect love drives out fear"* [2] and *"For God did not give us a spirit of timidity, but a spirit of power, of love and of self-discipline."* [3] This was the truth. I had embraced the lies of shame and fear.

Over the next several days, God continued to reveal other areas of my life where I operated out of fear. Though the list went on and on, I was filled with joy! God was revealing my core issues, and I expected all of my problems to start falling like dominoes.

One day I was so happy and giddy with joy that I playfully chased Janet around the pool table in our game room. It looked like a scene from an elementary school playground. Here is the boy chasing the girl with the girl laughing and saying, "Stop it! Stop chasing me!" I think Janet believed that I had truly gone insane! As I started to choose to walk in faith, life did get better. But fear was not my only issue. God still had a lot more to reveal to me.

The Way Out is Through

Then you will know the truth, and the truth will set you free.

- *John 8:32*

There was one positive during this dark time. I was driven to my feet in prayer. I do not mean my knees; I mean my feet. After Janet filed for divorce, it was impossible for me to sleep through the night. I have never experienced anxiety like I did during those initial weeks. I would eat dinner, drink a few wine coolers or a few glasses of wine, watch television, sip a few more glasses of wine and force myself to stay awake until my eyes were ready to slam shut. I would slip into bed and fall into a fitful sleep.

Unfortunately, the effects of alcohol would not last long, and my eyes would pop open after only a few hours. Once I was awake it was impossible to turn my brain away from my circumstances. I rehashed the last month before our separation, over, over and over again. Like a dog chasing its tail, I circled around with the same thoughts until I angrily bolted upright in bed and turned on the light. I tried to chase away the thoughts like a child chases away a bad dream, but this was no dream. It was reality, and it was maddening! At first I tossed and turned until the sun came up to start my day. After a few days of this insane pattern, I gave up and started walking instead of tossing and turning for hours on end.

Once my eyes opened, and I was sure I could not go back to sleep, I got dressed in the previous day's clothes and headed out into the dark and the dead quiet of the early hours of the morning. The first time that I walked through the back door of the motel, I was angry. I felt hot all over, and I walked at twice my normal speed. Each step was deliberate. Somehow I managed to be both quiet and make it outside in about ten seconds flat. I doubt if I had run if I could have made much better time. As I closed the door behind me, I heard the "click" of the door locking and was greeted by a blast of cold air. I was angry that Janet had lied. I was angry that I could not sleep. I was angry that I had no control over my circumstances. I felt completely out of control and victimized.

As I walked, I had no particular destination in mind. I felt like I was fleeing a hidden terror that was always just behind me. I wandered around the hospital grounds that were close to my hotel. Ironically, it was a hospital that specialized in heart attacks. I remember thinking, *At least when I keel over from all of this stress, I will be close to help.* The tightness in my chest was unbearable at times. I walked up and down the side streets until I felt my anger subside and I believed I could go back to sleep, even if it was for a single hour. The first few nights were pure anger release. The harder I pounded the pavement, the better I felt. That first night I must have walked five miles.

After a few days I was still waking up at about the same hour, but the anger was gone. Something was breaking. Instead of revisiting the injustice of the situation, I started to pour my heart out to God. Instead of aimlessly pounding the pavement, I started exploring further and wider. My sense of doom was lifting, and I was starting to get a sense of adventure, like there was something unknown yet exciting just around the corner. God was using the natural wonder and exploration of my unknown surroundings to pave the way for a supernatural adventure that He and I would take together. He was about to take me on a journey along a path not often traveled. I would need that sense of wonder and adventure in the weeks and months ahead.

The first few nights of my conversations with God were a pure monologue. I was speaking and sometimes yelling, and God was listening. I told Him how much I was hurting. I told Him that I felt like a complete failure. I was successful in the minor things in life, like work, but a dismal failure with the ones who really mattered, my family. Divorce had the strong potential to affect more than one generation, and I was now part of bringing divorce to our family history.

Eventually my monologue subsided, and I quietly talked to God and truly listened for answers as I walked the streets. I began to experience a peace that I could not understand. The anxiety lifted. My body felt more relaxed. I did not feel hot with anger or the same tightness in my chest. I started to live each day, each moment, for what it was, not for what I wanted it to be. I rejoiced in the little things, like when I spoke with a friend or when a meal that I had cooked turned out well, and I released the future into God's hands.

My circumstances had not changed. I was still living in a hotel. I was still getting a divorce, and I had no idea what to do. I had lost everything that truly mattered in this world. I was left with one thing of value and one thing only, God. For the first time in my life, I was ready for the truth even if its condemning finger pointed squarely at me. If God chose to speak, I was ready to listen. My life was a puzzle up to this point with no solution. I was ready for an answer, any answer.

The defensive noise of *it cannot be me* was fading from my life, and I was willing to listen. He spoke very quietly, but it was God's Spirit speaking to my spirit.

One of my first questions was about a pattern of avoidance that I was starting to recognize in my life. I recorded the following in my journal that night.

> *My dad [earthly] gave me some great advice when he taught me it takes more of a man to walk away from a fight than to be in one. But is this the root of my avoidance of conflict and my "peacemaker" role I constantly find myself in? How much of this is healthy?*

I was given a very gentle, "Yes, it is a problem." I had twisted my dad's advice from avoiding a bare-knuckle fight to conflict in general. I made it fit my need to create the perfect conflict-free world.

When a situation arose that had the potential for embarrassment, or where I did not have mastery of the situation, I was faced with two choices. Either I could endure it or avoid it. My primary coping mechanism was to endure. This came with its own set of liabilities. I could only endure so much before it drained my energy and left me exhausted, resentful, or both.

When I was at the end of my rope, I fell back on coping mechanism number two, avoidance. I never admitted my fears or apprehension to anyone, even to myself. I gave excuses, or I would ignore the situation until the time passed and the decision was made for me. Ignoring situations had become my favorite tactic of all time.

Another night (or was it morning?) God and I were talking about how I tended to operate with low expectations of others and myself.

Why do I do that [have low expectations of myself and others]? Is it truly out of kindness (somewhat no doubt)? Or is it so I am not disappointed? I know I like to surpass people's expectations. It takes the pressure off to "perform." So why do I feel that pressure in some areas of my life, and not in others? Does it go back to fear? In this case fear of failure? Search me oh God...."

Another quiet "Yes" from God's Spirit to mine. I feared any expectations around my performance. I preferred to go into a situation with people having low expectations of me, and then exceed them, than to disappoint. The shame of failure was so powerful that I set up an internal system of no expectations. If I had no expectations, I could not be disappointed. Just as important, if I did not have any expectations of others, how could they demand anything of me? It seemed like the perfect system, but it was a pure house of cards. It did not work well at all. Avoidance carried its own system of shame. I would tell myself, *you are so pathetic you cannot handle anything*!

Another morning I was sorting through why I was attracted to strong women. Most of my girlfriends, and ultimately my wife, carried an inner strength that intimidated many men. For some reason I was not intimidated. I felt a security with a strong woman at my side. Again, God provided the answer.

Too long since I journaled last [to] You. You reminded me this a.m. that I needed to write down fully what you have revealed to me about why I am (was?) attracted to strong women. There is a healthy side. I want a companion, a peer, not a puppy that follows me around. I am a collaborative leader, not an authoritarian. That's the healthy side. The unhealthy side, especially early in my life, was I felt completely inadequate as a leader! I did not want my wife to have to rely on my leadership because I knew I would fail her. There is that fear driven thing again!

I can still remember when Janet and I were discussing marriage that I told her I wanted a fifty-fifty marriage. It sounded and felt so affirming at that time. After all, women are just as capable as men. Why should there be a "one up, one down" relationship in marriage? The truth, as God revealed later, was that I wanted someone who would take care of me! I wanted more of a mother than a wife. When that desire was fulfilled, however, it created more shame in my life, more condemnation of failure as a man.

When God and I had those long conversations, the answer was not always "yes." There were times when I was raging against Janet and the unfairness of life in general. That is when I would experience His comfort. There was no sense of condemnation. There was no accusing voice of, "You can do better than that." He was letting me expend my emotional energy, pouring my pain out to Him. He was hearing more of my pain than my complaints. In Philippians 4:7 God promises a peace that passes understanding. I experienced that peace over and over again.

Scanning my journal, I see many other examples that I could give of what God revealed to me during that time. A few of the important ones are:

Remain open to reconciliation, but do not count on it.

Do not grow bitter toward Janet. You want to be able to sit next to Janet throughout your life (such as at your son's wedding) knowing that you do not hate each other.

Live your life now in ways that you can look back in twenty years and have no regrets. For me this meant to not go out and look for comfort in another woman. I was still married. Act like it.

As I write these words I am awe-struck at how God was at work in my life in perfect ways at the perfect time. It was by far the most lonely, painful time of my life. Yet at the same time, it was one of the best times of my life. I did not go through a single day tired or drained. Every walk brought me closer to the truth about myself and why my marriage had failed. As the days and nights unfolded, I began to see who and what was responsible. It was not all Janet's fault. I played my part, in fact, a big part.

The biggest role at this time was played by God, my friend and comforter. One of our pastors at our church recently said, "I have never gone one moment without being loved." I experienced and continue to experience God's love in amazing ways. At this time I could only feel a sliver of it, but that small portion was enough to sustain me.

Another significant insight came in November. My journal from that time says,

You [God] gave me a major revelation today of where I start the cycle in our marriage. My fear-driven life has driven me to unreasonably dig in [to stubbornly hold onto a position, refuse to participate in an activity, etc.]. This frustrates Janet to no end, but because she is aggressive she comes out fighting. I in turn become more defensive, so I come out fighting as well. In the past I've only seen where Janet's aggression started, not where my passive resistance drove her to frustration. I've always blamed her, when this particular cycle is ~~all~~ part my fault. Oh Lord, please forgive me!"

When I first penned this entry I wrote *"all"* my fault, but I quickly changed it to *"part."* I still was not at the place where I was willing to take full responsibility for my actions. Someone else had to play a part. Someone else had to share the blame.

When our children were growing up, my oldest son, Brett, would quietly taunt his younger brother, Josh, until Josh's frustration increased to the boiling point. Eventually Josh could not take any more, and he would punch his older brother, which would result in the cry, "Mom. Dad. Josh hit me!" My wife, who had vast experience with children from a decade of babysitting before we were married, taught me to ask the most important question before taking action. "Brett, what were you doing to your brother to make him want to hit you?" After I dealt with the aggressor, Brett, I would speak to Josh and help him understand that socking his brother did not solve the problem. Because overt aggression is easier to spot, it is all too easy to place the blame of a situation on the aggressive person and to completely miss the passive-aggressive behavior. This is exactly what I had done to Janet for years. My selfishness, stubbornness, defensiveness and a host of other issues were major sources of frustration to Janet. Like Josh, when she finally reached her breaking point, all of her pent-up anger and frustration came pouring out. It was then, like a child, that I would hold up my hands and say, "I did not do anything! What is your problem?"

At last, I had dropped my fearful guard of not being perfect enough to see a second symptom. I was passive-aggressive. I did not know the term at the time, but at least I was starting to see how my behavior was affecting Janet.

An Angel's Visit

Five weeks passed, and one day I received a surprise phone call from Janet. She asked me to come over where she was living at the time to talk. By this point I had moved back into our house, and Janet was living with a friend. I was not sure what to expect since she had cut off all conversation, and the only communication that I had with her was through our lawyers.

When we met she said, "I will stop the divorce, and I will wait twenty years for you to be healed, if that is what it takes, on two conditions. First, I want you to give me control of the money. I have lived for twenty-nine years feeling completely out of control. I believe that I am better with money, and I want you to know how it feels to have to trust me. Second, I need you to agree to meet with Gene and let him help you figure out what is going on." Janet went on to explain that she was now convinced that I would not become violent toward her or our family, and the potential of violence was why she had filed for divorce in the first place. I was relieved. I had no idea why she came to this conclusion, but I was grateful. It was truly an act of love. This did not mean that our (un)happy family was back together again. Janet was not about to make the mistake of putting us under the same roof until I had dealt with my issues. But at least there was a glimmer of a second chance. All right, a thousandth chance.

Her first condition was easy to accommodate. Ultimately, we decided to maintain the financial conditions of the separation. I agreed to the second condition, but I had some apprehensions. Although Gene was a trained and experienced family and marriage counselor, he was also married to Janet's sister, Carolyn. To top it off, I knew that Janet had talked to Gene extensively both before and immediately after our separation. Would he take her side? Would he have already formed his opinion "against" me? I was not sure.

Although her offer of waiting twenty years was generous, I was not about to take that long. I wanted to get to the bottom of my issues and get fixed! The problem was that I still had no idea what was driving me deep down inside. I had some answers, like fear, shame and passive-aggressive behavior, but they were all symptoms. Symptom chasing is a lot like squeezing a balloon to prevent bulges. Squeeze it flat in one place, and it will bulge out somewhere else. This was my life. As I started to deal with fear, I became shameful of all the places I was fearful! Controlling my emotions only led to more exhaustion. The more exhausted I was, the more that I avoided those prickly, uncomfortable situations. It was maddening!

Janet offered one of her free airline tickets for Gene to come and spend some time with me. This was amazing in and of itself given our separation. What was even more amazing to me was that Gene was more than willing to take time out of his busy schedule to fly in from San Antonio, Texas to spend the weekend with me. His attitude was a sharp contrast to the "not bothering" mantra that had permeated my family.

The shock of the pending divorce, the sleepless nights and miles upon miles of walking and praying in the early hours of the morning had brought me to the place where I was willing to entertain that I was part of the problem. I sincerely hoped Gene could help me get on track. I was both excited and fearful about Gene's visit. I wrote in my journal the morning of his arrival,

Well Lord, You have brought Gene here to help. But how? I have emotions that are mixed with anticipation (breakthroughs)

and fear (Is Gene biased?). Please calm my fears and heighten my anticipation! In reading through my notes I still have some open questions about myself. Why the need for perfection? [How does Your revelation fit as to] why I am successful at work, but not in marriage? Lord, today is the day I must see one of two things; either I am the absolute demon Janet presents me to be, or her perception is way off! Please bring the truth to light Lord. We're stuck where we are until You [reveal the truth]. This is the scripture He gave me…"In my anguish I cried to the Lord, and he answered me by setting me free." (4)

I had no idea how prophetic that verse in Psalm 118 was to my life at that moment. I was not willing to settle for peace at any price. I was not willing to accept band-aids where I knew deep surgery was required. The real beginnings of freedom were just around the corner.

Angels are God's messengers. Gene truly turned out to be an angel, but in the flesh.

Arrested Emotional What?

One of the first activities Gene performed when we sat down together was a Genogram (5) of my family. I knew very little about my grandparents. All but one had died before I was born. I did not have much knowledge about my dad's brothers or sisters because, as a family, we never had much contact. It was the same story for my mother's family. But when Gene and I discussed my dad, I could have spent hours describing his stories and our time together.

Finally Gene asked about my mother. I had to be honest with him. I only had a handful of real memories of my mother. For Gene, that was revealing.

Only a few relationships play a significant role in our development as children. Our parents are at the top of the list. The fact that I had so few memories of my mother only had two potential reasons. Either I had painful memories that I had blocked, or she was absent from my life. In my case it turned out to be a combination of both.

Gene spent a great deal of time probing and confirming his suspicions about me. Because Gene and Janet had already spent hours talking about our relationship, Gene had a working hypothesis when he arrived at my house that he needed to confirm. He suspected that I had Arrested Emotional Development, or AED.

There are five core wounds that can lead to AED. They are:

- Abandonment (rejection or neglect), real or perceived
- Incest
- Molestation
- Emotional abuse and
- Physical abuse [6]

The core wounds that each of these forms of abuse can lead to is the same lie; *there is something wrong with me*. If the child internalizes these lies, they conclude that they are flawed and unworthy of love and respect.

Some types of abuse are easier to identify, like blatant sexual, verbal and physical abuse. The husband who beats his wife to a pulp after a drunken binge is obviously an abusive husband. Other forms of abuse are more subtle and can be hard to identify within a family system because it may be the family, or even societal norm. Still, abuse is abuse.

Gene showed me the "Power and Control" wheel [7] pictured next to help me identify areas of abuse in my own life, and more painfully, to see where I was abusive toward Janet. Acknowledging that I was the recipient of abuse was hard enough. It meant that I had to shatter the illusion of parental perfection that I had created. However, that was nothing compared to looking at my own behaviors as abusive. Me abusive? If there was abuse I was the victim. How could I be both the victim and perpetrator?

The possibility was absolutely gut wrenching to me. If I look carefully at that original copy that Gene gave me, I can still pick out where the teardrops began to fall on that piece of paper. Deep down inside I knew Gene was right. I had been abused, and I was an abuser. I had a lot to learn, and I was ready. I was also ready to change.

Gene identified two of the five core wounds in my life. Both occurred very young. One of them started while I was still in the womb.

Physical Abuse is any touch that is not given in love, respect and dignity

Emotional Abuse is any communication, admonition, reprimand or reproof that does not uplift, edify, or bring conflict resolution

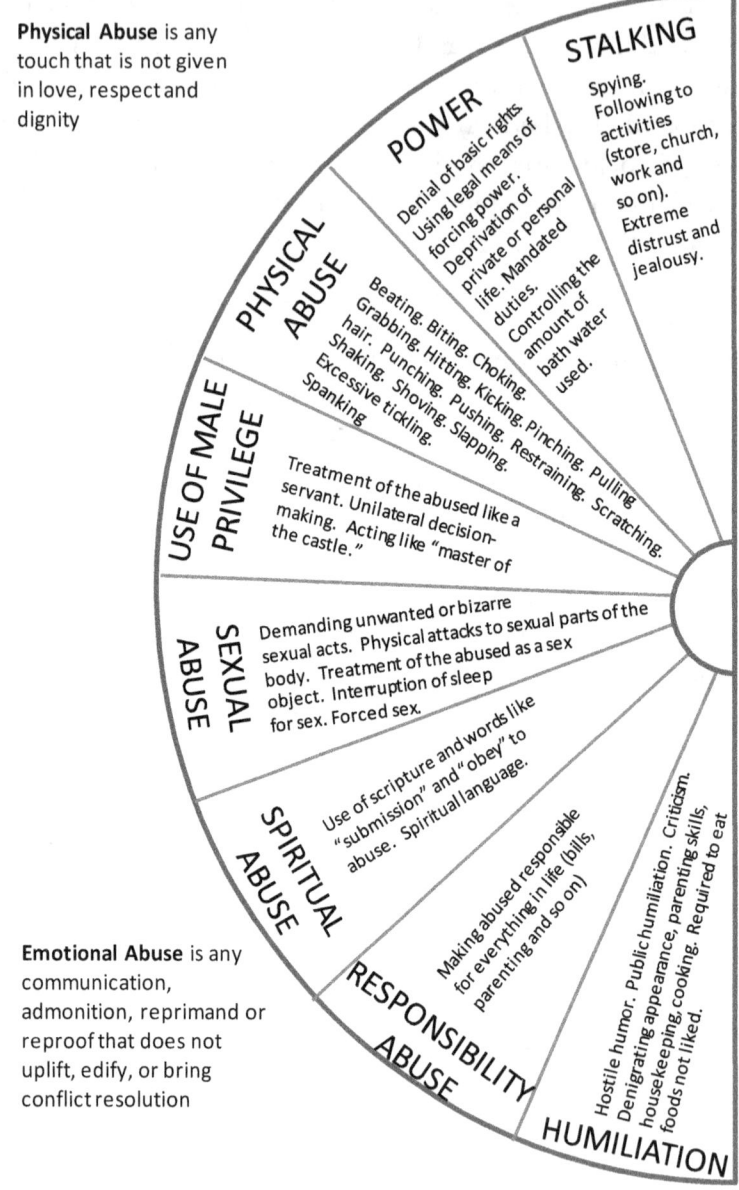

POWER
Denial of basic rights. Using legal means of forcing power. Deprivation of private or personal life. Mandated duties. Controlling the amount of bath water used.

STALKING
Spying. Following to activities (store, church, work and so on). Extreme distrust and jealousy.

PHYSICAL ABUSE
Beating. Biting. Choking. Grabbing. Hitting. Kicking. Pinching. Pulling hair. Punching. Pushing. Restraining. Scratching. Shaking. Shoving. Slapping. Excessive tickling. Spanking

USE OF MALE PRIVILEGE
Treatment of the abused like a servant. Unilateral decision-making. Acting like "master of the castle."

SEXUAL ABUSE
Demanding unwanted or bizarre sexual acts. Physical attacks to sexual parts of the body. Treatment of the abused as a sex object. Interruption of sleep for sex. Forced sex.

SPIRITUAL ABUSE
Use of scripture and words like "submission" and "obey" to abuse. Spiritual language.

RESPONSIBILITY ABUSE
Making abused responsible for everything in life (bills, parenting and so on)

HUMILIATION
Hostile humor. Public humiliation. Criticism. Denigrating appearance, parenting skills, housekeeping, cooking. Required to eat foods not liked.

Power and Control Wheel

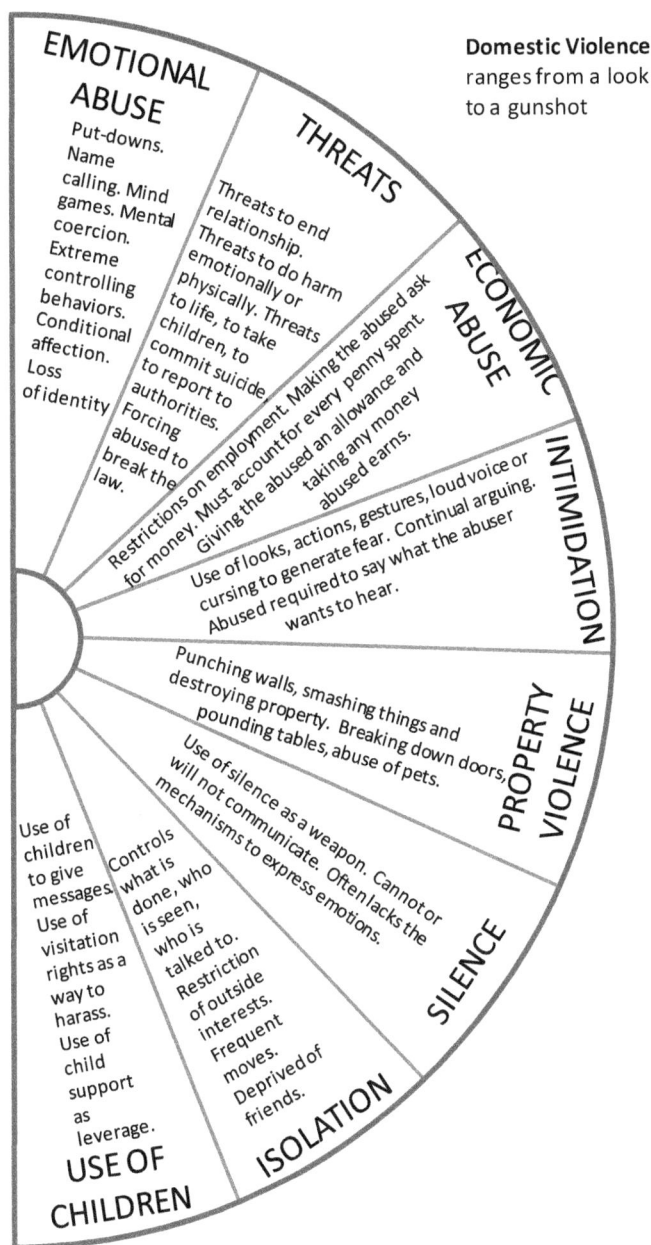

Domestic Violence
ranges from a look
to a gunshot

EMOTIONAL ABUSE
Put-downs. Name calling. Mind games. Mental coercion. Extreme controlling behaviors. Conditional affection. Loss of identity

THREATS
Threats to end relationship. Threats to do harm emotionally or physically. Threats to life, to take children, to commit suicide, to report to authorities. Forcing abused to break the law.

ECONOMIC ABUSE
Restrictions on employment. Making the abused ask for money. Must account for every penny spent. Giving the abused an allowance and taking any money abused earns.

INTIMIDATION
Use of looks, actions, gestures, loud voice or cursing to generate fear. Continual arguing. Abused required to say what the abuser wants to hear.

PROPERTY VIOLENCE
Punching walls, smashing things and destroying property. Breaking down doors, pounding tables, abuse of pets.

SILENCE
Use of silence as a weapon. Cannot or will not communicate. Often lacks the mechanisms to express emotions.

ISOLATION
Controls what is done, who is seen, who is talked to. Restriction of outside interests. Frequent moves. Deprived of friends.

USE OF CHILDREN
Use of children to give messages. Use of visitation rights as a way to harass. Use of child support as leverage.

Paul Hegstrom and Life Skills International, Inc.

The Wound of Abandonment

I was born in 1959 in rural Indiana. We lived on a farm, although we were not farmers. We rented the house while my dad scratched out a living as the owner of an electric motor manufacturing plant. I did not know that we were poor. I did not know that other kids had meat more than twice a week and that only beans was not a normal meal. I did not know that other people had more than one car and they did not wait weeks or months to get the television fixed. To me, we were normal in every way.

My dad had the work ethic of many men who lived through the Depression. His father was a "dirt farmer" in the summer months and a coal miner in the winter. My dad left home when he was sixteen years old and went to the city to make a better life for himself and, ultimately, his family. The first winter away my dad slept in a family's basement and shoveled coal into their furnace for his room and board.

Getting ahead in life took hard work, and my dad worked hard at a myriad of jobs. He was a professional boxer, worked as a salad chef at the Brown Derby (which is where he met my mother) and he ultimately worked a series of odd jobs as he labored toward his degree in Electrical Engineering. It took him twelve years to get his degree, but he stuck with it while raising his family. After some time at General Electric, he gathered investors and started his own company. This took hard work and long hours. In his mind providing for his family was of paramount importance. It took priority over his wife and my two brothers, so much so that neither of my older brothers really knew my father well.

My mother was forty-three when they conceived me, much to the shock of both of my parents. Perhaps it was ignorance, but Dad believed that she could not get pregnant once menopause started. Surprise! Here I came! My mother had heart problems during the pregnancy, and by the time I was born, she was not strong. Having already raised two sons, now fifteen and twenty years old, she was tired of parenting alone because of my dad's workaholism, and she was just tired in general. When I was born she told my dad, "I raised the other two. You raise this one." Those words were to have a profound impact on my life.

As a result most of my memories are of my dad. He taught me how to drive a car by sitting on his lap. I was four or five years old when he would prop me up and let me drive the car down the driveway. He taught me how to swim in the creek near our home. He took me to work where I found an endless array of fascinating places to explore and things to do in the shop where the motors were manufactured. He always praised me for my intelligence and how grown up I always acted, which made me try all the harder to act more grown up and mature. I was his "little man," and he was my perfect dad.

Most of the memories I have of my mother are of her in the kitchen. Some of my earliest memories are of her cooking, but most are just of her sitting, smoking a cigarette, reading a newspaper or organizing her "green stamps" which she used to get the essentials we could not afford to buy. Was the kitchen her hiding place or her sanctuary? Unfortunately, I will never know in this life. The one thing I do know is that the reason I have very few memories of my mother is because she was not a nurturing force in my life. She was Missing In Action (MIA).

Now, as an adult I can look back on those times of my mother's emotional absence, and I can understand her pain. She did not feel well. She had minor heart problems throughout the years that ultimately culminated in a major heart attack that ended her life just before my eighteenth birthday. She was probably severely depressed for many years, taking Valium, which was common in the 1960's. We lived in the country in my early years and had only one car. Because my father worked all of the time, this left her isolated and alone. Both of my sisters-in-law remember her as being unhappy for many, many years.

When I think of my mother now, I think of a woman who loved me, and I loved her. Adult eyes bring adult perspective. But what was my perspective as a child? This is where my problems start. She just was not there. That was the reality. As a young child, I believed her absence had to be because something was wrong with me.

In the morning my mother fixed my breakfast and sent me out to play. I played alone all day, either in my room, exploring the house, or outside in the barn. I took things apart, and I even put them back together on occasion. I kept myself busy. I do not remember longing for companionship. Being alone was normal. When I returned, I typically found my mother in her usual spot in the kitchen. She never physically neglected me. I never froze in the Indiana winters, and I never starved; she just rarely did anything *with* me.

I listened for my dad's car to come driving down our gravel driveway every day. When I heard the crackling sound of the car approaching, I ran to the door and greeted him as soon as his feet entered the house. He never pushed me away and was always overjoyed to see me. We were inseparable through the rest of the evening. I would even sit on his lap to eat dinner many nights.

We lived in that Indiana farmhouse until I was six years old when my dad lost the motor manufacturing business. It was not a typical business failure. There were plenty of customers. My dad had sublet the manufacturer of one of the components to a third party, and they were failing in the field. Honoring the warranty, my dad virtually bankrupted the business. He was a man of integrity, and integrity demanded he uphold his word, no matter what the consequences. This ultimately forced him to sell the business to clear the debt. We were now out of a business, and he had to find work. That work turned out to be in the neighboring state of Ohio.

I did not find out until years later that my dad never sought my mother's counsel on that move. He just announced that we were moving. The decision was made. My mother went but not without repercussions. To get back at my dad, she knowingly threw away important things that later needed to be replaced. It was her personal, private rebellion. Of course, I did not know any of this was taking place at the time. All conflict took place behind closed doors. All I knew was that we were moving somewhere for some reason, and it would be great. My dad said so, and I believed it.

The Wound of Sexual Abuse

After we moved to Ohio, I at last had friends. We lived in the suburbs, and there were kids everywhere! It was a sharp contrast to the isolation that I experienced back in Indiana on the farm. I had one friend in particular, Larry.

Larry and I would hook up after school or on the weekends and would ride our bikes far and wide. We explored the creeks that were filled with fossils, catch crawfish in the summer, ride our sleds in the winter, play baseball or football and just hang out in general. For a kid who had been completely isolated the first six years of my life, this was heaven.

I was shy, but not a recluse, so smaller groups of friends felt comfortable. Larry, a few friends and I just hanging out together made for many a perfect day. But by the age of seven, Larry and I had a dark secret.

Sexual experimentation among boys is considered "normal." But this was far from normal. We had frequent sexual encounters, sometimes two and three of us at a time. I have dim memories of one or two other boys joining us in an abandoned barn on the outskirts of the small town where we lived. I cannot remember their names or their faces. I never told anyone about those encounters for many years. I felt permanently soiled, like a dirty rag that needed to be discarded. I believed if anyone knew, I would be rejected. Even more troubling was the belief that I deserved it.

This all started around the age of six when a male babysitter taught me how to masturbate. I also remember neighbors, an older girl and boy across the street, who invited me over to look at their dad's pornography together. After that everything is a blank. My memories jump from those early memories to frequent sexual encounters with other boys. In all likelihood there was at least one episode of more severe molestation, but I have no specific memories, only the evidence of my own behavior. It is like looking at the road after a car accident. You see the skid marks and the broken glass and conclude that there was an accident. Six or seven year olds do not know about intimate sexual contact. They have to be shown. It has to be experienced. The conclusion of my counselors is that I was probably severely molested, although I have no conscious memories of the event.

During this time I was both repulsed and drawn to my sexual behavior. It held both deep shame and great excitement. It took many years before I admitted my past to anyone. It is no wonder that I was highly protective of my sons as they grew up. I wanted to be sure that they had every opportunity to experience a pure and unmolested childhood.

I pulled out of my homosexual behavior right before my teen years. Over time I had a growing sense that what I was doing was wrong. It did not take me long to turn my attention from sex with boys to a sexual interest in girls. My sexual encounters with girls were isolated to kissing and light petting in my early teen years. The first time that I had true vaginal sex I was fifteen years old. I was never a "conqueror," and I had a true disgust for guys who used a girl purely as an object to satisfy their sexual desires. However, every steady relationship I ever had included frequent sex.

Arrested Emotional Development

Gene explained to me that it only takes one of the core wounds to create the fertile ground for AED. Just because I was abused did not condemn me to a life with AED. It was how I chose to internalize those events that led to my emotional illness. My major symptoms were:

- Irrational fears
- Control issues
- Self-care issues (others had value, not me)
- I attacked Janet, not the problems (I could not be wrong)
- Lack of personal responsibility (isolated to Janet)
- Sexually stunted (something always felt "wrong")
- Relationally stunted, lacking intimacy

- Deep sense of shame and worthlessness

Once, Janet found my oldest son crying when he was about ten years old. Janet asked Brett, "What's wrong?" in her kind and caring way that a mother does so well. Brett answered, "I'm not ready to be a man!" He was only ten years old, so of course he was not ready to be a man! Somewhere along the line I made the same proclamation. I did not feel adequate or prepared to be an emotionally mature adult. I became emotionally frozen in time. My childhood coping mechanisms followed me into adulthood and became a way of life. Like Peter Pan, I never grew up.

In AED you can emotionally mature at most two years past your core wound. Some level of emotional abandonment occurred even prior to my birth, so I was really young when it came to significant relationships. My sexual wounds occurred when I was around six or seven years old. As a result I was emotionally-sexually a nine year old. It is no wonder that Janet protested in times of frustration, "You are acting like a seven year old!" Her assessment was not far off.

My list of issues felt long and daunting. Fortunately, there was a simple, but frightening solution. I had to choose to mature in all the areas of my life where I was emotionally and relationally stunted. Gene, man-to-man, gave me permission to grow up. He told me that I had to take responsibility for all areas of my life. Nothing is "someone else's fault." This point was, and is, critical to me. Nothing is "someone else's fault." I cannot control others, but I can control myself. I had to learn to be assertive with Janet, not passive-aggressive. And the last is the most important point of all. Janet was my wife, not my mother!

It felt like I was jumping off a cliff with no bottom in sight. Every fiber of my being cried out, *you cannot do this. You will not survive this!* Fortunately, prior to Gene's arrival, I made the decision to trust and believe him. Every one of the solutions I tried for the last forty-nine years failed. Gene was a professional. God was clearly leading me to answers up to this point. Unknowingly, I was taking an important step. I was choosing to trust someone other than myself.

Solutions of the Child Become the Problems of the Adult

When I was a child, I talked like a child, I thought like a child, I reasoned like a child. When I became a man, I put childish ways behind me.

- 1 Corinthians 13:11

If you are now an adult, you were once a child. As far as I know there are no exceptions to this rule. Part of the maturing process is putting "childish ways behind." You will not find many adults begging their spouse in the grocery line for a candy bar and crying because they do not get what they want! Adults just do not behave that way. They have left that childish behavior behind...far behind.

However, one does not always operate as an adult in all areas of your life just because you have an adult body. This was certainly true of me. Because I was emotionally stunted, there were definite childhood coping mechanisms that I carried into adult life. Because I had an adult intellect, I was able to creatively refine these mechanisms to the point that they were acceptable, even right, to people who were not closely involved with me. But if you could have seen through my thin veneer, you would have seen a hurt and frightened child that hid behind the mask of the adult. One of the major areas where I lacked maturity was in true intimacy.

Lack of Intimacy

We all need nurturing throughout our lives. However, the nurturing a child requires is very different than the needs of an adult. A child needs a protector, a guide, someone who will tell him/her that no matter what happens it will be all right. As a child if you fell down and scraped your knee, you would melt into the arms of your mother who would scoop you up and kiss your "boo boo." You knew that she could "make it all better."

Since I experienced emotional abandonment, I yearned to have my unmet childhood nurturing needs fulfilled. I wanted to be praised and appreciated. I wanted someone to want to spend time with me. Most of all I wanted to be loved unconditionally. The problem was that I had a child's version of those needs, not an adult's, so Janet could never fulfill them. In my desperation I had a series of emotional affairs with other women. Because of my emotional immaturity in this area of my life, the relationships with other women were not based on sexual attraction. I was attracted to women who were strong nurturers and who were long on mercy and short on confrontation or judgment.

It was not unusual for me to hang out with the women in the kitchen when we had dinner with friends. This was not a conscious decision. I did not say to myself, *Greg, your nurturing needs are not getting met. Janet cannot meet them. Go spend time with other women and maybe that will satisfy you.* Somewhere deep inside me I felt drawn to their company.

I never crossed the sexual line, so I never felt guilty about my behavior. In my mind I had a number of friends, and some of them just happened to be women. It was only by God's grace that I never had a physical affair. My behavior was an indicator of a deep wound. Affairs are not about sex. They are not even about the excitement. They are about attempting to fill a deep need in our lives.

My needs were never met no matter how many women, or what kinds of women, were in my life. There was always emptiness in the relationships, even with Janet. I felt like a prisoner who was only given enough food to stay alive. I enjoyed the time when I was with a woman, but once the house was quiet and I was alone with my thoughts, the same feeling of emotional emptiness crept over me. Whatever emotional connection I received, it was never enough. I was back where I started. Empty.

Janet and I never experienced true intimacy in our relationship. I was not capable of operating as a peer in a husband-wife relationship. I viewed Janet as a vastly more capable and emotionally stronger person than I. I was the weak one who needed nurturing and protection. It felt like I was being forced to operate in a grown-up world. I pushed myself to do what I needed to do, retreating wounded and exhausted from everyday life. I thought that this was normal and what everyone experienced. Like a buoy that has broken free from its chain and is adrift in the ocean, I was my own point of reference. I looked confident and in control on the outside, but on the inside I was dying.

Now that I understand more about AED, the reason is obvious. I am no longer a child, and Janet is not my mother.

Understanding the difference between my wife and my mother was vitally important to my healing. Some of the key points that were important to me are illustrated in the following table.

Wife	Mom
She is responsible <u>with</u> me	You are her responsibility
She is someone to cry with	You can cry on her shoulder
We depend on each other	You depend on her
I am her protector, not her controller	You are protected by her
We will always love each other	You will always be loved by her
We make love to each other	You never make love to your mother!

As a child, the relationship of a mother to a son is a relationship of a superior to a subordinate. It is a relationship of a "big person" to a "little person." The relationship between a husband and a wife is a relationship between equals, and I was not operating as an equal partner with Janet. I was the child, and Janet was the adult.

Because of my AED I wanted Janet to fulfill the needs that only my mother could have fulfilled. I yearned to be unconditionally loved and taken care of by a mother. Unfortunately, that was impossible. I was now a man, and I needed to transition away from the needs of the child to the needs of the adult. By growing up emotionally, I was setting the stage to have my real, adult needs met in healthy ways. As my adult needs are embraced and met, my childhood needs fade into the background.

Control

When we moved to South Carolina at the age of ten, we were once again in the country, and my dad surprised my mother with a new car so she would not be stranded while he was at work. If this was not the first new car we owned, it was one of the first, and my mother was thrilled. It was a gold Chrysler New Yorker. I can still remember the immense back seat of that old Chrysler. I could stretch out to sleep and still have room for toys piled all around. The first major victory over my parents in the control game took place in that very back seat.

We were on a long trip and stopped at a restaurant for lunch. When I looked at the tables of the other people eating and saw all of the variety of food, I was filled with excitement. We normally packed some kind of sandwich for our trips, so eating at a restaurant was a major treat. We were sitting in the restaurant when an older couple, probably around the same age as my parents at the time, came over to the table to talk to them about their grandchild. That grandchild was me!

I can still remember the deep embarrassment that I experienced about having such "old" parents. It felt like the entire restaurant was looking at me. I wanted to disappear. It was an easy mistake to make. My mother was forty-two when she became pregnant with me. Both of my parents were in their fifties by the time this incident took place. I did not say anything at the time. I remained the perfect child, smiled, greeted the other couple as expected, and finished my lunch. I could not wait to get out of the restaurant and away from the prying eyes of others. The embarrassment was unbearable.

As we continued to travel, when the time came for dinner, I lied and said that I was not hungry. I quietly insisted that I did not want to come into the restaurant and they could just go ahead and eat. I was not willing to risk a repetition of the earlier embarrassment.

A verbal battle ensued. It was not a nasty fight. There was not any name calling or yelling. My parents calmly insisted that I come in, and I, with equal calmness, resisted. They eventually gave up and left me in the back seat of the car to sleep while they satisfied their growing hunger. Of course I did not sleep. I reveled in my victory. As soon as they went back into the restaurant, I sat up and grinned from ear-to-ear. I had passively thrown a rebellion and had won!

I was not only in passive resistance, but I lied to get my way. I feigned not being hungry. It was less painful for me to be hungry than to be embarrassed.

I never matured beyond this very immature coping skill. I did not learn to be assertive; I learned to get my way through passive resistance. When Janet reached the ultimate point of frustration with me she would say, "You are stubborn all the way to China!" This passive-aggressive pattern became a well-refined and dominant coping mechanism for me in my marital relationship. Hand-in-hand with passive-aggressive behavior was my coping mechanism of avoidance.

Avoidance

When I was about thirteen years old, my hair was long and blonde. Well, it was mostly blonde. Because I spent so much time in the swimming pool, the chlorine gave my hair a slight greenish tint. It was not very noticeable, and I was not self-conscious about it until we were in church one Friday night. A couple of women sitting directly behind our pew took the time during the service to analyze why my hair was so long, and why it was green! I was devastated. I froze like a statue, and my hearing tuned out everything else that was going on around me. I honed in on their every word. It felt like everyone in the room was now looking at me. I felt small and severely flawed. If I could have run out of the church without causing a scene, I would have.

This is a delicate age where physical imperfections take on the mental proportions of the state of Alaska. A single pimple feels like a giant, red volcano sitting in the middle of your forehead! I responded just like I had in the restaurant incident. I calmly suffered until after communion, then I headed straight out the back to talk to the priest. I hoped that he could somehow magically remove the pain that I was feeling.

The priest tried to reason with me as a young adult. He tried to help me find perspective. Because of my emotional age, I just could not get there. I left discouraged and convinced that I needed to find my own solution to the problem. With adult eyes I can see that the women were the ones with the problem. However, for me, the problem became associated with the church, so the church was the place to be avoided.

I was a compliant child. Blatant rebellion never occurred to me at first. I was not able to avoid the whole church service, but I could avoid part of it. Immediately after communion was the perfect time to get away. We would file right past the back door, and when we did, I bolted straight out.

It was not long before I started my campaign of not going to church at all. Eventually my parents gave up and left me at home alone. It was years before I set foot in a church again. I had nothing against God; it was His people I could not stand!

This passive avoidance became a pattern of my life. If there was an activity that I did not want to pursue because I felt it would result in embarrassment, I found a way to avoid it. If I felt overwhelmed by our finances, I would not balance the checkbook. If there was somewhere I really did not want to go because I did not feel capable, I found an excuse, any excuse, not to go.

In many areas of my life, I pressed through the feelings of inadequacy or embarrassment and just did what needed to be done in spite of my feelings. This was especially true of my work where I felt like I needed to grow and stretch. Work was one place where I felt comfortable, and I did not feel like a failure. Another area was activities with my sons where I felt that my avoidance would hold them back in their growing into the kind of men I wanted them to be. I knew I had unreasonable limitations, and I did not want my sons to be shackled by the same chains that I carried. Inevitably, even in those times, I would expend so much mental energy pushing through my embarrassment or fears that I ended up exhausted and without the energy to function well for days or even weeks.

Emotional Shutdown and Withdrawal

As children we are not equipped to process extreme emotional pain. We rely on the significant adults in our lives to help us work through the pain and confusion of everyday life. When left alone to process these emotions, we often bury the feeling deep inside. This is how I chose to handle my feelings of rejection and loneliness. I pushed the pain beyond the access of my conscious mind.

Not long after we were married, Janet told me that I was an emotional "flat liner." My highs were rarely very high, and my lows were rarely very low. I held my emotions as close to the middle of the road as my abilities allowed. I did not know it at the time, but it takes energy to suppress emotions. The stronger the emotion the more energy it takes to suppress it, lest it rear its ugly head and betray me. When that energy runs out, the emotions come pouring through the gap like the water through a break in a dam. I either felt angry, or I shut down all together. In most situations I shut down.

My suppression was so complete that I did not consciously "feel" the extremes of emotion. When my mother died, I felt very little. I cried a bit at the funeral, and tears would occasionally come, but I did not grieve her death until many years later.

After Gene left I started to see a therapist, John, who specialized in AED. One of the first things John did was to hook me up to biofeedback to gauge my emotional response to his questions. A common occurrence during our sessions was for John to interrupt the flow with the question, "What was that?"

My normal response was, "What was what?"

John had noticed a strong emotional response to a question or a line of discussion, and I did not notice a single thing.

The first time John made the simple request, "Tell me about your mother," I registered the highest emotional response that the machine could record! What did I feel? Nothing. What did I notice? Nothing. I was completely emotionally numb and out of touch with a key tool which God had given me to live a healthy and happy life, my emotions.

Anger and Offense

When I could not hold in my emotions any longer, I would erupt. I did not gently move from calm, to agitated, to angry. I went immediately from calm to off the chart! I was like a corked bottle building up pressure. I exercised every ounce of self-control within me until it was completely exhausted, then I would explode. I was not physically abusive toward Janet, but I was extremely verbally abusive. Words were my weapons, and I could wield them with great accuracy. I was not concerned with hurting Janet. I thought that she had already wounded me. I often thought, *at least I didn't hit her,* as a rationalization of my verbal abuse. In truth verbal abuse can leave wounds just as deep as physical abuse.

I honestly believed that nearly every response toward Janet was in self-defense. In my mind I was the victim of a carefully planned attack designed to wound or humiliate me. In truth Janet would simply ask an innocent question like, "Have you taken out the trash?" or "Did you balance the checkbook?" I would erupt because I could not handle my brittle shell of perfection being challenged.

To stop the pain I experienced from the perceived rejection, I resorted to verbal attacks that set Janet back on her heels. My highest priority was not to solve the problem but to stop the shame that I experienced with failure. I went into a mindless state where my only goal was to prove Janet wrong. I rarely remembered what the argument was about. Janet would accuse me of not tracking the conversation. I honestly thought I was tracking it completely, when in truth all I could remember was the pain of the perceived attack. I had the memory of a goldfish, about three seconds!

The end was nearly always the same. If I "won" the argument, I felt vindicated but horrible. I knew the emotional carnage to both of us was far beyond the offense, yet I did not know any other way. I would try to be as kind as possible to Janet because I knew we both were hurt. It was, in my mind, her fault that things had regressed to the point that they did, but still, I was her loving husband, and I would love her even if she was wrong.

The Strange Case of Dr. Jekyll and Mr. Hyde

In Robert Louis Stevenson's novel, *The Strange Case of Dr. Jekyll and Mr. Hyde*, Stevenson creates a vivid portrayal of a split personality where one is intrinsically good and the other evil. [8]

I was not the same person with Janet that I was with everyone else. Because I had "mommy" issues, any concern or disappointment, real or perceived, that Janet displayed toward me, triggered a desperate response. I literally felt panic sweeping over me. If Janet was unhappy, I reasoned it must be because of something I had done. If we argued I would win at any cost because to be wrong meant to be imperfect, and to be imperfect meant that I would be rejected. I lived in a constant state of fear of failure. Janet's description of my Jekyll-Hyde behavior is insightful.

Greg's "mommy" issue showed itself at many different turns. Oftentimes I would receive my best attention from Greg when I was sick. However, when I was sick with bronchitis, my voice would get deeper as I got more miserable. Greg would go off on me, aggressively defending himself and attacking me with false accusations. I would beg him to stop, saying, "I do not feel well! I am not attacking you. Please leave me alone!" Though I never met Greg's mother, I knew her smoking may have deepened her voice. After many years, I hypothesized that maybe there was some "mommy" issue going on with Greg.

In a medical emergency, Greg was usually wonderful, giving me lots of attention. However, the one time that I was actually at death's door, Greg went to work, took care of the kids and generally avoided spending much time at the hospital. I was left to fight for my life alone. At the time I did not think about who was at my bedside. However, when I finally came home, he was sharing with some friends about how he did not think I realized just how close I came to dying. I thought to myself, of course I knew, but it was not evident by Greg's choices that he knew. It seemed the closer I came to death, the less Greg could watch. Going to work seemed like a better answer than watching the saga unfold at the hospital.

One night, after battling for my life for six days, I asked Greg to come be with me at the hospital. I'd had too much painkiller, and for days I was experiencing either sleeplessness or motion nightmares that would scare me awake. I was exhausted so the doctor ordered a sleeping pill for me. Since I was afraid I might be trapped in a deep sleep, having scary nightmares all night, I begged Greg not to make me take the pill alone. He responded that he was tired and that he was just getting into bed. No way was he going to come to the hospital. I was so scared. Rarely did I show this kind of vulnerability. I had put up an incredible fight to live and here was my husband denying me the one thing I needed. I needed him! I needed his arms to hold me. I needed my husband who had said, "I love you deeply" to show up. He did not, and I faced that trial alone.

Whenever Greg did anything wrong, he would lie about it but in a very believable way. He could forget his actions in a split second. It was strange how a man that took pride in his integrity could be so far from it with me. He would walk a mile to return a dollar if he was given the wrong change, but he would lie about any behavior that was less than perfect with me.

Greg could get so defensive. Everything was about being "right." Whoa, if he was not perfect! It was impossible for him to acknowledge he was wrong. It was as if his very life depended on his being "perfect." He would take me down verbally slicing and dicing, accusing me of using a threatening voice, saying, "You do not know how you sound," "You don't realize how cutting your words are," or "You are so mean and hurtful," anything but accept that he was wrong. This was often confusing because, for me, it was not about being right or wrong. I just wanted to know if something had been done. I was not a parent asking. I did not look at Greg like a child answering my questions. I did not know what his problem was. I just knew that the inconsistency was not fun to be around, and the real Greg, the man I fell in love with, was kind and fun at heart. Greg was Mr. Nice and Mr. Not Nice. He was Dr. Jekyll and Mr. Hyde.

When Janet was growing up, she had a sister, Peggy, who discovered the secret hiding place for the cookies in her house. She was not satisfied with just eating a single cookie or two and sneaking away. She, in true childlike fashion, decided to create her own private stash and proceeded to stuff her pockets full of cookies. Her mother noticed the dark brown crumbs around her mouth and asked, "Peggy, did you eat some cookies?"

Peggy responded without a single hesitation, "I didn't eat any!" and quickly placed her hands over her pockets! She continued to protest, "I didn't put them there. I won't ever do it again!" as her mommy took her down the hall to face the consequences.

I still laugh when I hear that story told at family gatherings. It is the classic "hand caught in the cookie jar" scenario. Of course, Peggy was only six years old when she tried to cover her imperfections. I was an adult doing the same thing. You can almost hear me saying, "I did not do it. It was not me. It was you!" I had to be right. I had to be perfect.

There was a second dynamic taking place within Greg "Hyde" Tilford. I often did not feel that I was up to the task. I avoided the hospital when Janet was desperately ill because I felt completely overwhelmed by life. I was exhausted by the time Janet called and asked me to come and stay with her. I thought that it was a completely unreasonable request. I was the one taking care of our two boys. I was working a full day, every day, so I stayed employed to keep that all-important insurance that was providing for Janet's care. I was the one living and balancing real life. Janet's only job was to lie in a hospital bed. I completely failed, however, to meet her emotional needs because emotional needs were not real to me. Suck it up and push through it. That is what I did, and that is what I expected Janet to do.

I also knew, deep down inside, that there was a real possibility that I was going to be raising our children alone. I was afraid that I would fail. Like the myth of the ostrich that sticks its head in the sand when danger approaches, [9] I avoided dealing with the severity of Janet's condition by limiting my time around it. If I did not see it, it did not exist.

The Healing Process

In his poem, "A Servant to Servants," Robert Frost penned an often-quoted passage.

He says the best way out is always through.
And I agree to that, or in so far
As that I can see no way out but through—
Leastways for me [54]

This theme has become the mantra for counselors all over the world. It was shortened a bit to, "The way out is through." The pain that I avoided all of my life had to be faced. There was no alternative. The way out of the pain was through the pain. I lived in a fantasy world. In this world I was perfect; my past did not affect me. I was in control, and it was all Janet's fault.

In every journey there are always choices to make. The journey that I was on was no different. I only had two choices. I could ignore all that God had revealed to me directly and through Gene and others, or I could lean into the pain. I knew "the way out is through," but the possibilities that were ahead terrified me. What if I was the demon that Janet portrayed me to be? What if I was worse? Could I live with myself? Would I become suicidal when I looked in the mirror without the mask of false perfection? I thought that I could handle it, but then again, was that just another self-delusion that would dissolve like a mirage in the desert? I honestly did not know, but I knew that I had to find out. The truth was that I was a failure in everything that I valued most in life. I wanted to be able to truly love and care for my wife. I wanted to be a great father, and one day, grandfather. At this point I was a mess, and something had to change.

Why Traditional Marriage Counseling May Not Help

I struggled whether to put this topic first in this section or last. I do not like starting a positive journey with something that appears so negative. However, if you have ever thought, "I've tried to get help from friends, pastors, and counselors, but nothing worked. I would take advice from our pet hamster if it could talk. I just want someone to tell me what to do!" then read on. All right, you may not have thought of getting advice from a hamster, but if you have been through traditional marriage counseling, and it did not help your marriage, this section will encourage you.

AED is still not well-recognized in counseling circles unless physical abuse is involved. Even then many counselors focus on stopping the behavior instead of attacking the root of the problem. Janet and I experienced this more than once.

A healthy marriage requires two emotionally healthy adults who are able to work together to resolve their differences and solve their problems. When dealing with AED, at least one person in the relationship is not emotionally mature. In this case I was that person! This meant that traditional counseling would not work. Every attempt we made to get help failed. In fact, it almost always made the situation worse. Janet is going to take the lead on this section.

Our First Counselor

In our seventh year of marriage, we started seeing our first counselor. Kathleen tried to get us to fight in front of her. There was no way Greg was going to show his true self, so I matched his example. If he was going to stay above the fray, I would stay there with him. If he was going to be polite and calm, I decided I would as well. Still, she could tell I was reacting a lot.

One day she asked to meet with each of us alone. She asked me to read a paper out loud that was a description of a wife saying that she loved her husband so much and could not ever say no. She would take "it" and take "it" and never say, "No More." This wife was battered and verbally abused, and her husband was an abusive alcoholic.

After I read the page, Kathleen said, "Janet, that is you." I could not relate to the woman in the story at all. I always believed that if Greg would hit me, I would have a legitimate reason to leave him. What Greg did to me did not feel equal to physical abuse. It felt more like a not so amusing amusement park. I was stuck perpetually riding the roller coaster and the merry-go-round.

I told Kathleen that I could not relate. It felt like she just wanted me to trust her *carte blanche*. I felt pressed to agree with her. She was the professional, but I swore if Greg ever physically hit me, I would have left. What part of this story was me? I just could not see it.

When Greg met with Kathleen, she told him, "Janet must be hard to live with." That made his day! He was now even more empowered against me. I was totally confused. I had tried to describe what was going on at home, but now I felt betrayed and helpless. It was devastating to me personally. I became very leery of counselors. We spent money that we did not have to get a marriage that was worse than ever.

The Marriage Renewal Weekend

After fifteen years of marriage, we were invited to join our pastor at the time and his wife at a Marriage Renewal Weekend. A few weeks before the weekend, we were each given a survey to fill out separately. It consisted of situational questions. Since this was my busiest time of year, teaching swimming ten hours a day, I was tired. I did not like any of the choices. My attitude was really poor about it. I hated being put in a box. I did not care one way or the other. I could not figure out how this questionnaire was going to help our marriage. I was full of cynicism and doubt, frustrated and hopeless.

The weekend began just hours after I completed the summer swimming lessons. Six weeks and one hundred fifty children later, "I had left it all in the pool." I arrived at the retreat exhausted but exuberant to have completed another season of lessons. I was willing to be there in order to improve our marriage, but I was definitely weary.

During the introductions, the couple leading the weekend announced they would visit our rooms later that evening with the results of our questionnaires. They arrived at our room around ten thirty, just as we were giving up on them and preparing to go to sleep! They said that they wanted to start with Greg. As soon as they began, I knew that I was in trouble. He had aced the whole thing! I sat in fear, knowing I was next, and if something did not happen soon, like the floor swallowing me, they were going to reveal just how messed up I was. I knew Greg would relish the moment!

They suggested a few areas he could improve on. However, overall, he came off looking like Mary Poppins...practically perfect in every way.

I watched carefully as they brought out my graph. Immediately, I could see that the drawing of my results were the exact opposite of Greg's. If his were high, mine were low, over and over. Inside my heart sank. Greg was appearing as a positive and hopeful person; I looked like a depressed and hopeless wreck. The woman proceeded to take me to task. With such a great husband, I should be grateful and happy. The life threatening events that I had gone through three years earlier and the surgery to remove one of my thyroid lobes containing a tumor two months before were showing up all over my answers. I was hopeless, and I was sad. Considering I had the practically perfect husband, why wasn't I the happiest of wives? What had me so upset? I felt set up. Then her husband said something very kind, "Janet, I see something in your eyes that tells me you are a survivor and that you are going to make it."

The hour they stayed was horrible. I could not wait before they were gone. Then Greg took over where they had left off. For the next three and a half hours, Greg lectured me on how much he agreed with her and how I was in denial. He kept repeating, "You are never satisfied. Nothing satisfies you. You always look at the things that are wrong. Finally, Janet, you have to own this. You are a very unhappy person. I've been trying to tell you for years, but you just won't listen to me."

I was devastated. The anger that I felt filling out the questionnaire was now replaced with hopelessness. I would never get to be right, even a little bit. Greg was perfect, and I was not! Submit, try harder, let go of my needs, stuff more, be less vulnerable by sharing less of my heart with Greg...I sure had my work cut out for me. The rest of the weekend, I began to make my plan for surviving in this marriage. I would never, ever put myself in front of any counselor with Greg. I would never take that risk ever again. He was impossible to compete with. I always came out on the losing end. Why spend more money just to get hammered? I had plenty of that at home.

My spirit was crushed. The weekend was very devastating to our marriage. Not only were we not on the same page, but the more we tried to solve our problems, the further apart we became. Within two years after that weekend, three of the six couples' marriages ended in divorce. Here we were about to be a statistic, too.

Empty Nest Counseling

Around the twenty-fourth year of our marriage, with Brett married and Josh in South Carolina at college, we were experiencing more and more time as empty nesters. I began to realize how much of a buffer our sons' presence had been. Greg's false accusations increased, and he became more and more certain of his rightness. When the boys were home, they defended me, or they pointed out to Greg how I had really spoken. They would clarify what I meant or what I had actually said. With them out of the house, defending myself was a losing battle. We grew farther and farther apart. The accusations against me increased. A year after Josh went to South Carolina, I told Greg I wanted him to leave.

Greg went to our pastor who suggested we go to a marriage counselor in the church. I had promised myself never to get in a counseling situation with Greg ever again. I believed I would end up on the losing end, and our marriage would be no better. If Greg could get me in front of someone, he would come off looking like Mr. Wonderful and, once again, become more empowered. Greg begged me to just come and tell the counselor what I was experiencing.

I reluctantly agreed but warned him that I would not be available for a cross examination. Greg said that he sincerely wanted to know what he was doing that was hurting me so badly. I decided to once again believe that he really did want to know.

The counselor agreed to meet with me on the terms that I had given. I was not going to engage in the "he said, she said" anymore. At first the counselor asked Greg some questions about family history, which he answered. When the counselor began to turn his questions toward me, Greg interrupted to correct me. The counselor turned back to Greg and asked, "Is that the way you usually speak to Janet?" Greg said yes. The counselor responded that he thought Greg sounded like he was talking to a seven year old, not a wife.

Later the counselor returned his questions to me and asked, "What is your main complaint?" I began to tell him about the false accusations and how when the boys had been at home they were a buffer for me. Again Greg interrupted to say that the boys had requested not to be brought into the situation and that I was not honoring their wishes.

The counselor looked at Greg and said, "That was not what Janet was doing. Janet was only addressing how the boys have been a buffer in the past and now that they are not there, she believes your accusations have intensified. You are bringing up your sons now and their desires to be left out of your situation." Greg was stunned. He was totally off his game plan. I could not imagine how this was going to go. It felt great to see him squirming, trying to cover himself, only to have the counselor continue to track the truth. I could not help but be delighted. Twenty-five years of being under the spotlight. I felt a little giddy. I could have stood on the couch and cheered! This was a big moment! A really big deal!

For me, this was the first time someone had caught Greg in his semantics, false accusations, circular arguments, belittling and demeaning me. I was shocked and thrilled. The counselor continued to lean into Greg for the next few sessions. At home, Greg stopped the false accusations.

After a few weeks the counselor began to try and focus on me. I refused to go there, believing that I would get ripped apart verbally and emotionally at home if I allowed my shortcomings to be brought up in front of Greg. Throughout our twenty-five years, Greg had never provided a safe place for me to be wrong. My imperfections were fodder for him. I am easily trusting and transparent, so resisting the counselor and Greg was a difficult and huge stance for me.

During the first session the counselor asked me why it had taken me twenty-five years to say, "No more!" I had seen the problems very early in our marriage. Through the years I busied myself in the church, striving to be a godly woman. Was I as mean and as angry as Greg believed that I was? I pursued personal development in Bible studies and with Klemmer and Associates. I learned to take responsibility for my choices and practiced telling myself the truth. Years of delving into my anger issues greatly defused my temper. Still, the frustrations of being in a relationship with Greg left me in a constant mess of confusion. One minute he would say that I was great, and the next minute he would decry me as the meanest person that he had ever known.

For six months Greg stopped making false accusations, and we got along well. Then suddenly the behavior came back. I looked at him and said, "If you can fix it for six months, you can fix it forever."

He then fixed it for another six months, and I began to think "It" was truly going to be gone this time. But a year later it came back strong, and he was more empowered than ever. I suggested going back to the counselor since he had helped Greg with "It" in the past. Greg refused because I had not allowed the counselor to work with me. He said that the counselor had wanted to deal with me, but I would not cooperate.

Greg was right. I was not going to go back to marriage counseling for me. I knew that I was making great progress in my life, and I knew that Greg was back to his old ways. For some unknown reason, Greg's fixes were always temporary. In twenty-six years, no progress had been made. Life with Greg was crazier than ever. Circular arguments, semantics, false accusations. It was all so confusing. I wore myself out trying to track it all, arguing for the truth and burying the pain. He was known for being a man of immense integrity, but he could disassociate himself from guilt, like Superman, faster than a speeding bullet. He could not be wrong.

What Went Wrong?

It looks like I was setting Janet up for failure. I was not. I was patiently waiting for Janet to get fixed so I would no longer be under the microscope, and we would have the amazing marriage that we had always wanted. Sure, I had my flaws, but I believed they were minor compared to the anger and resentment that Janet carried. I believed my lies, and I believed them deeply. Every time we went to a counselor, in the end I looked like the victim and Janet the perpetrator. They assumed that they were working with two emotionally healthy individuals. They were only half right.

There were other dynamics that led to us not getting the help that we needed. When Janet and I first started attending counseling, it was over twenty years ago. Very little was understood about AED at that time, and in fact even now, the awareness is still fairly limited. Also, there is a tendency to symptom chase; if you are fighting, then the solution must be to learn to fight fairly. Unless the counselor works toward finding the root of the behavior, the symptom chasing can last a lifetime with no real healing ever taking place.

What Was Going on with Me?

In my case, a focus on changing the behavior only led to more frustration. I still had the same fears and coping mechanisms operating deep inside. When attending counseling I was being asked to operate "normally" in spite of my feelings. I believed the only solution was to try harder. I thought this is what everyone did. I tried with all my strength and self-discipline and things improved in our relationship for a season.

Then my strength and self-discipline would erode. I became emotionally exhausted. The earlier episode Janet described where I spent days in the back bedroom of her sister's home is an example of where I was totally and completely emotionally spent from everyday living. This is when things became worse than ever for Janet. I just did not have what it took to operate in spite of my feelings any longer. If Janet asked anything of me, anything at all, I responded in anger, verbally attacking her until I got what I wanted; I just wanted to be left alone.

As long as I was stuck in AED, I was incapable of having a normal adult relationship with Janet. It was not about our marriage. In fact it was never about our marriage. It did not make any difference how much we learned to "fight fair" or what listening skills we developed. These were all helpful to our marriage, but not healing. I was still driven by the wounds deep inside me.

What the counselors were trying to do was not wrong. If we had both been emotionally healthy, all we would have needed were a few tweaks here and there, and we would have been on our way to a healthy marriage. The problem was that I was still stuck in AED, and I was still convinced that Janet was the problem. After all of the counseling, I knew what to do, but I was completely incapable of sustaining it for any length of time. I was an actor on a stage. The changes were only skin deep.

How Do Children Think?

In his book, *Broken Children, Grown-Up Pain*, Paul Hegstrom describes how the solutions of the child can become the problems of the adult.

> *A child who is under the age of puberty is lacking the chemicals in the brain to see the whole picture and make decisions. So the wounds that happen in childhood, a time during which the child does not have the capacity to understand, trigger the thalamus at the point of the wound to keep the child from being hurt again.... Once a child is traumatized, the child will be more vulnerable to perceiving future events as trauma.*

> *The child without the chemicals in his or her brain is a child in the age of directives, not the age of decision. And when [the apostle] Paul says bring down the strongholds and bring captive the thoughts (I Cor. 10:5), that requires a decision. Choosing to think positively instead of negatively requires a decision. But the wounds of childhood have locked the child in the age of directives, where the child is unable to make decisions...the thalamus makes the decisions.*

> *As the child grows, the unresolved trauma locks him or her into a survival mode. The child's emotional development is halted, and he or she develops survival techniques instead of changing.*
> (10)

Adults are able to make a decision to act in spite of their feelings. For example, they can override their fear response and consciously put themselves in positions of danger. This is how a policeman can patrol a dark alley or a soldier can charge into battle with bullets flying and mortars landing all around. Adults respond to the various situations in life. On the other hand, a child in the same situation will probably run for cover! God's protection mechanism for children who do not yet have the reasoning powers for such decisions is *reaction*. It is a good thing. However, when carried into adulthood it becomes a liability.

The time of directives is an important time in the life of a child. It is a time where we are learners, not leaders. If a parent tells us that we have done something wrong, we feel remorse. If we are praised by our mother or father, we feel great. We do not evaluate whether the praise or rebuke is right or wrong. Since it came from the most significant adults in our life, our parents, it is right, true and just. This is the way things work in a healthy family environment. It does not take perfect parenting to make God's plan for raising a family work. When the family is not emotionally healthy, childhood wounds can take up deep roots and can affect us for the rest of our lives.

For example, what happens if, like in my case, mom is MIA? It must mean that there is something wrong with *me*. I must have done something wrong, or worse still, there must be something wrong with me that makes me unlovable. As a child I did the only thing I knew to do; I tried harder to make my mother happy with me. All I understood were directives. I became the perfect child. I tried to always be helpful, always courteous and always kind. No matter how hard I tried to be perfect, however, I was never perfect enough. I lived with constant disappointment in myself. I felt like a failure. Again, my only conclusion was that I must be severely flawed. It was at this point that something very strange happened. I became emotionally frozen in time. I became arrested in my development.

It Looks All Wrong, But It's All Right

The problems that I was experiencing in my marriage and in my life, were not marital problems. They were the result of my long buried pain. This meant that the secret to my healing lay with me, not Janet. She may have her own issues to work through, but like mine, they are not about the marriage.

After Janet stopped the divorce, we started to occasionally talk and reconnect. One of the difficult decisions that we faced was when to live together again? It seemed like we were on our way to answers, so what was stopping us? It came down to what was best for us, and in particular me, rather than what we wanted. Neither of us wanted to be separated. Neither of us wanted there to be deep emotional issues to work through that could take years, but the reality was that there were. Knowing the problem is not the same as being healed from it. If a doctor tells you, "You have appendicitis," you will not say, "Thank you, Doctor. That is what I wanted to know. Have a good day!" Your next question will likely be, "What time is the operation?" Unfortunately, I was still at the point that every time I thought "Janet" I subconsciously thought "mother." I was far from being healed.

We had to take a sabbatical from one another for a season until we reached the point where we were healthy enough to work on our issues *together*. Janet coined the phrase "Marriage Recovery" for this period of the separation. I like the phrase because it truly captures the spirit and intention of the time apart. It was very different from the first part of our separation. During the first phase we were both letting go of the old marriage. It had to die before something better could be reborn in its place. This phase was so that we could once again reunite in a healthy relationship. This was not a decision that we made in a vacuum. Gene has worked with many men throughout the years with my problem, and the solution is the same. Grow up emotionally. Growing up takes time.

Now it was time to truly get down to business. I was committed to the healing process. I had professional help from John to assist me in getting there. The way out of the pain was through the pain, and I was willing to endure anything to reach the point of healing. I was no longer doing it for someone else. I was doing it for me. I knew it was what God wanted, and it was what I desperately wanted.

Shame

My early realization of how fear was driving me prior to the separation provided some relief, but a much deeper work was still needed. The next stop on my journey was healing from shame. Lynne Namka describes shame as

> ... a fear-based internal state of being, accompanied by beliefs of being unworthy and basically unlovable. Shame is a primary emotion that conjures up brief, intense painful feelings and a fundamental sense of inadequacy. Shame experiences bring forth beliefs of 'I am a failure' and 'I am bad' which are a threat to the integrity of the self. This perceived deficit of being bad is so humiliating and disgraceful that there is a need to protect and hide the flawed self from others. Fears of being vulnerable, found out, exposed and further humiliated are paramount. Feelings of shame shut people down so that they can distance from the internal painful state of hopelessness. [11]

I had no idea of the power that shame held over me until I read an article by Ms. A.J. Mahari on abandonment. [12] There was one sentence that pierced my armor and went right to the core of my soul.

> *Whatever caused you to develop BPD[2] was not your choice and was not your doing, at all. You did not choose to experience and/or perceive the core abandonment that you experienced that left you with so many unmet primary needs that arrested your emotional development....You did not create the circumstances in your past that caused you so much harm, before you were even two years old.*

The first time I read that statement, I just stopped and stared. I read it again, and tears started to dot the paper. I rolled out of my chair and onto the soft carpet of the floor. I sobbed on the floor in a fetal position for at least forty-five minutes. Years of guilt poured out of me. I had believed the lies that, "I am bad," "I am a failure," "I am flawed," and "I am worthless" for so many years that the truth that it was not about me at all went straight to my soul. It washed over me like a flood. The feelings of condemnation were cracking.

I cried out in between the sobs, "It's not my fault. It's not my fault!" I have never cried like I did that day, and I have not cried like it since. When I finally stood up in my living room, the sun was on its way down, and darkness was descending over the room. However, a light was burning in my soul! Something amazing happened when I embraced that truth. I was set free from the lies of shame. I still had to fight to hold on to that truth in the days and weeks ahead, but the stronghold was broken.

---

[2] BPD stands for Borderline Personality Disorder. AED is part of the family of BPDs.

Did this mean that I was not responsible for my actions? Was my verbal abuse of Janet someone else's fault? Absolutely not. I did not cause my wounds, but I am responsible for how I responded to my own wounds. Ms. Mahari goes on to say

> However, you and you alone are responsible, as an adult, for your life, regardless of your past. When you can admit this, sit with this and understand this, you can make new choices to recover from your past. [12]

I was not responsible for what was done to me. The abandonment and sexual abuse were not my fault. I was a child. I should have been protected, but I was not. What was done to me shaped me, but it need not define me. I was not doomed to be a product of what was done to me. I was discovering that I was so much more. What I was responsible for was my response to those hurts.

The Root of Shame

Shame runs deep. In fact it may be the deepest of all of our wounds. What causes shame? Condemnation. [13] The word rings with finality. It has the connotation of the pronouncement of a criminal sentence. You can almost hear the judge say, "Sir, you are condemned to a life living out your existence as the worthless human being you are." There was no room for negotiation, no process for appeal. The good news was that for me, as a Christian, condemnation is a lie! In the book of Romans, Paul tells us

> Therefore, there is now no condemnation for those who are in Christ Jesus. [14]

What an amazing statement. No condemnation.

- Jesus told the "sinful" woman, "Your sins are forgiven." [15]
- Jesus told the paralytic, "Take courage, son; your sins are forgiven." [16]
- Before his death, Jesus said, "This is my blood of the covenant, which is poured out for many for the forgiveness of sins." [17]
- The Apostle John wrote to the Christians at the time, "I write to you, dear children, because your sins have been forgiven on account of his [Jesus'] name." [18]

Jesus was condemned for you and me so that we can live life as free men. The Great Judge of the universe has declared us not guilty!

The amazing thing is that Jesus was and is there to meet me. Most importantly He is there to forgive and receive me.

Yet to all who received him, to those who believed in his name, he gave the right to become children of God. [19]

Jesus hears our cries. Like prodigal sons returning home, our heavenly Father will not just receive us. He will run to greet us! [20]

I love the picture Joseph Prince paints of our forgiveness. He calls it a "waterfall of forgiveness." [21] It is an amazing picture of continuous, total, complete cleansing. It does not matter how dirty I am. If I stand under a waterfall, it will not take long for every bit of dirt to be washed away. The same thing is true of God's forgiveness. It is total. It is complete. It covers my past sins, my present sins, and yes, my future sins. It leaves no grounds for condemnation. I am free from condemnation…forever.

I had mouthed and quoted those words for years. Now I was truly living them. There is no longer any basis for condemnation. I know the truth. The truth has set me free!

Now that you know the secret of my freedom from shame and condemnation, it is time to cover some specifics on how I put that freedom into practice.

Self-talk

Thoughts are powerful. To think is to create. We are all constantly creating. We continually change our environment with our thoughts. Just the simple thought, "Pick up the glass" changes a room. It is a small change, but if the glass is full of grape juice, the carpet is white and children are playing Nerf wars, it may result in a large change! I also shape myself by the way I think. [22] Because all actions start with a thought, my thoughts, especially about myself, are incredibly important. Let's take a real-world example.

Janet says, "Greg, will you take out the trash?"

I answer, "Sure, Sweetheart, I'll be happy to!"

The next day:

Janet asks, "Greg, did you take out the trash?"

At this point I realize that I completely forgot to take out the trash. Even the stench rising from the kitchen was not a clue. I have three possible responses.

Response 1: My condemnation takes over,

"I do not know why I always have to take out the trash! Why can't you just do it?"

A pure reaction. No conscious thought involved. I did this more times than I can count.

Response 2: My self-talk kicks in,

I think to myself, *Man, I am worthless! I cannot do anything right! I sheepishly answer, "No...."*

My eyes are downcast. I slink away. I may or may not take out the trash. Another common response in my life.

Response 3: My simple solution,

"I'm sorry. I forgot."

I stop what I am doing and go take out the trash. No condemnation. No negative self-talk. I simply solve the problem.

The first two responses are unhealthy. The last is where I now land, but let's spend some time on the middle response, response number two.

I am declaring to myself (and declarations are powerful statements) that because I am human, and I forgot something, that my entire being is flawed. That is what the statements "I am worthless" and "I cannot do anything right" imply. The punishment (character assassination) does not fit the minor infraction (not taking out the trash). This is typical of shame.

Some of my typical self-talk when I was in the depths of AED started like this.

- You are such an idiot…
- You are worthless…
- Why would anyone want you?
- You cannot do anything right…
- No one will love you…

They are all lies.

Fear

God clearly revealed to me that I had huge issues of fear. As men we are not supposed to live in fear. We are naturally protectors. We are the ones who look in closets in the middle of the night and scare away the monsters from our children's dreams. When looking for an intruder, we grab the baseball bat and fearlessly creep through the house when our wife says, "Honey! Wake up! I heard a noise!" But the truth is at those times we are afraid. We override our fears to do what needs to be done. We are men. And men tackle the hard jobs in spite of our fears.

But what if those fears run deeper? What if those fears are with us every day? What if we wake with a sense of inadequacy, knowing that we are really fakes? I felt like a child in a grown-up world. I felt inadequate as a parent. I felt inadequate as a husband. I felt inadequate as a lover. I had an almost constant sense of fear. It was not directed at anything in particular. It just hung over me like a dark cloud. But I would have never given it that strong of a name. I would say I could be "a little apprehensive" because that was the full extent of the emotion that I experienced at a conscious level, but that apprehension drove me to avoid normal, everyday situations that emotionally healthy people tackle with ease.

How did I tackle my fears? First, Gene gave me permission to grow up. Adults make their own decisions, but children need permission to do something substantial or out of the ordinary. In a way Gene was addressing that part of me that was still a child and saying, "I am a man and an adult. I am giving you permission to step out from where you are and start an amazing adventure. You can grow up." This allowed me to start moving forward in the areas of my life where I was frozen in time. Second, I began to stop hiding my fears and to talk about them with my counselor, John.

The day that I went to our local health club and signed up for a membership was a huge sign that I was breaking through. I had always avoided going to work out in any public place because I felt physically inadequate. I had a puny weak body. I felt that way when I weighed one hundred twenty-five pounds, and I still felt that way when I weighed one hundred eighty pounds. I was also afraid of looking like I did not know what I was doing. The first was a lie, and the second was the truth! But an almost magical transformation took place in my life.

I felt a little apprehensive when I walked into the health club, in truth this time, but I was not paralyzed with fear! The first thing I did was sign up for a run-through of the equipment. This solved the problem of not knowing what I was doing. The solution was simple. The real victory took place while I stood, in all my naked glory, and changed clothes in the locker room. I did not feel ashamed! There was no stuffing down fear or apprehension. I did not need to tell myself, *you can get through this*. I even stood there for a minute just looking around shocked at my own lack of reaction. I simply changed into my workout clothes, went upstairs and started the training on how to use the equipment. Sweet victory!

This was not the only victory I had over fear. My earlier list of fears included things like:

- Do not get into an argument!
- Do not "fail" in sex!
- Do not lose any money!
- Do not let others see you as you really are!

I do not experience paralyzing fear in any of those situations any more. As I faced each one, I was able to process my feelings ("the way out is through"), move through the previous lies and move on. I still have healthy fear (I am afraid to jump off a building), but most of my unhealthy fears have melted away.

Perfectionism - I Am Not God

The statement *I am not God* seems fairly obvious, but when I felt like I had to be perfect, that is essentially what I was saying. I believed that there were only four people I could absolutely rely on. They were me, myself, I and God. In that order. Part of being an adult is accepting our limitations. John Bradshaw writes

> *Healthy shame [also called guilt] is the permission to be human. To be human is to be essentially limited. It is to be finite, needy and prone to mistakes. Healthy shame lets us know that we are not God and that we truly need help.* [23]

What a freeing statement! It means that when I am not perfect, it is more than all right. It is human. When I out and out fail, it is not the end of the world. It means that I am human. Even more than that, it means that I do not need to reluctantly receive a Savior. I can welcome Him! I can say, "Jesus, I need you," with all the joy and freedom in the world. He is God, and I am not.

John Bradshaw summarizes this sentiment as

The first three steps [in the 12 step program [24]] restore the proper relationship between ourselves and the source of life. Admitting powerlessness and unmanageability, having faith that a greater power can restore us to sanity, and making the decision to give up control and submit our will to the care of God ...restores us to our healthy shame [remember, this is guilt] and grounds us in our fundamental humanness. The shamelessness, grandiose control madness and God-playing are given up. [25]

He is God, and I am not. And I am glad. I am free to be human.

Sexual Abuse

I find it odd that although abandonment can do the most emotional damage, sexual abuse carries the most shame. A simple truth set me free from the shame around my sexual abuse.

It was not my fault.

I did not do anything to attract being sexually abused. There is nothing wrong with me. I was a child, and children should be protected. But because we live in an imperfect world, I was not. Often violators are someone known and trusted by the family, and they betray that trust. They were wrong. I was not. They had a problem. Not me. It was not my fault.

The emotions around sexual abuse are complex. God intended sex to be an expression of love, trust and intimacy. When that natural order is broken, especially in a young child, feelings are awakened at an age when the child is incapable of processing them. What God intended to be tender may have been painful. What God intended to be voluntary, a giving of one's self, was forced and therefore, taken. And most importantly, the feeling of intimacy, sex is the most physically intimate act between two people, was disassociated from love and respect. The most intimate act was turned upside down. There are a number of possible responses to sexual abuse. In his book *Victims No Longer*, (26) Mike Lew lists a few of the issues that can arise from sexual abuse.

- Loss of memory of childhood
- Loss of healthy social contact
- Loss of the opportunity to play
- Loss of the opportunity to learn
- Loss of control over one's body

The list could go on. The recurring theme is loss. These are not losses that take place during the act. They are losses that come as a result of the shame and isolation from sexual abuse. This is another instance where the solutions of me as a child, to internalize and hide, became the problems of me as an adult. What are some of those false solutions? Here is a partial list of emotions and their outworking from Mike Lew's book. (27)

- Shame
- Anger
- Guilt
- Fear of expressing anger/difficulties
- Need to be in control
- Need to pretend that I am not in control (helplessness)
- Fear of intimacy
- "Avoidism"
- Pain and memories of physical pain

- Compulsive eating/not eating/dieting/purging
- Self-abuse

This is another list that could go on and on. The responses are many and varied. I experienced all of them.

Is Healing Possible?

Even after so many victories, I read the list and doubt crept in. I asked myself the question, *is full healing and recovery even possible?* I found the answer to be a resounding yes!

Again, I found the thoughts of Mike Lew to have tremendous insight:

All too often men attempt to reason their way into denial and minimization of abuse. They "think" it really wasn't so bad, or the pain they are feeling isn't so terrible. They are hesitant to take the next "logical" step toward understanding their situation, fearing what might be stirred up. A vitally important step for male survivors is letting go of the following myths:

myth 1: Vulnerability = Weakness

myth 2: Rigidity = Strength

myth 3: Comfort = Safety

myth 4: Under Control = In Charge

Many men talk about being "afraid to be vulnerable," as though vulnerability were some hideous flaw. Fearing what might occur if he were to allow himself to be vulnerable--what uncontrollable destructiveness would be unleashed, what dire aspect of his character could be revealed, what further abuse he would open himself to—the male survivor seeks to maintain tight control over his emotions and behavior. [28]

Interestingly, this is the one topic I had opened up about over the years. As a result I already processed a lot of the sexual abuse in my life prior to counseling. It no longer carried significant shame or emotional energy. What I did not recognize was the effects of the abuse on the rest of my life. Like ripples in a pond, the sexual abuse in my life sent waves to every shore. I did not connect any of my fears or avoidance with the sexual abuse.

There were other steps that I had taken over the years that directly correspond to Mike Lew's recommendations in his book.

Break the secrecy – Mike recommends that you tell at least one trusted friend exactly what happened to you. Janet was the first adult whom I ever told that I was sexually abused and about my sexual behavior as a child. Years later some aspects were still haunting me, so I shared my experience with a friend and elder at our local church. I entered that conversation with fear and trembling! I was completely caught off guard by his response. Instead of condemnation, which is what I expected, I received compassion. He said, "I was sexually abused, too."

I was shocked by his response. First, because I did not receive the rejection that I expected when I shared my deepest and darkest secret, and second, that he was a victim of sexual abuse as well. I thought I was nearly alone in my experience. The truth is that it is estimated that one in six boys are sexually victimized before their eighteenth birthday. [29] If you were sexually abused, you are far from alone.

One of the keys to breaking the strength of a lie in our lives is to tell someone else. This is especially true in the case of sexual abuse. Once it was spoken, what was done in private, what I had kept secret, no longer needed to be hidden. Its strength was broken!

Later as I worked with small groups of men in our church, it became a shockingly recurring theme. In one group, four out of the four men were sexually abused as children! I was not alone. In that group of four men, three had never told another human being about their experience until that day.

Stop the isolation - I am not talking about physical isolation. I had friends that I shared activities or hobbies with. Those were surface relationships. I took the risk to "go there" with others that I trusted in my life. I did not need to talk about my sexual abuse with everyone, but I had to open up with a few trusted friends. I needed to be real and to be vulnerable.

Get professional help – The road to healing for sexual abuse can be complex, but it is achievable! I got a professional to help me with my journey. Theophostics, a Christian inner healing ministry, traditional counseling and plain healthy friendships were all integral parts of my healing. I had to learn to give myself these gifts.

The Accuser

There was an external source of the lies and shame as well. It was the whispers of the enemy of my soul, the devil, satan[3] and his minions. In the Bible satan is called

> ...*the accuser of our brothers, who accuses them before our God day and night* [(30)]

Yes, just as there is a real God, there is a real devil. He does not like me. In fact he hates me. The good news is that, as a Christian, he has no power and no dominion over me. The book of James tells us

> *Submit yourselves, then, to God. Resist the devil, and he will flee from you.* [(31)]

In the book of Mark, Jesus did an amazing thing.

> *Calling the Twelve to him, he sent them out two by two and gave them authority over evil spirits.* [(32)]

The "evil spirits" were demons. And lest you think that the authority Jesus gave them was something special just for his twelve closest followers

> *The seventy-two returned with joy and said, 'Lord, even the demons submit to us in your name.'* [(33)]

Yes, we have authority over satan and his followers. Jesus defeated him at the cross, [(34)] and he gave us the same

---

[3] I never capitalize any of the names of satan. I do not want to suggest that he has any equal footing with God, even at the grammatical level.

authority. This means that we have the right and ability to tell satan to take a hike! I was struggling with taking this authority when a friend and counselor at our church told me his practice.

Michael told me that every morning he proclaims out loud, since satan cannot read your mind, "I am under the love and protection of my Lord and Savior, Jesus Christ. satan, you have no place in my life, in my home or in my day. Leave now, in Jesus name!" There is nothing magical about the words. It is not a secret prayer. It simply speaks a truth. satan has no hold on us. Proclaim it!

I have already given satan more press than he deserves. However, there is one more point. Most of the condemning thoughts that ran around in my head were not the direct whispers of the devil. He may have planted some of them long ago, but once I adopted them as truth, they became mine. It is a lot like spinning a top. Once I give it some momentum, it will spin a long time on its own. The lies of condemnation were planted long ago, and they were still spinning around in my mind because every time I acknowledged one of them as truth, I added a little momentum to the lie.

Stopping the Lies

Though it sounds hopeless, it was far from it. The solution was to stop taking my self-talk as truth and to run it through the filter of "no condemnation" before I acknowledged it in my life. This meant paying attention to my thinking at a conscious level. I believe this is what Paul wrote when he said,

We demolish arguments and every pretension that sets itself up against the knowledge of God, and we take captive every thought to make it obedient to Christ. (35)

In war, all captives are not the enemy. However, they must be interrogated carefully to find out where their loyalties truly lie. This is what I had to do and continue to do with my thought life. I take my thoughts captive and give them a thorough interrogation!

Some of the lies became easy to spot, such as, "You are worthless!" Once I spotted them, I paused my thinking and then declared the truth. Going back to the example of taking out the trash, I restate the lies of, "I am worthless! I cannot do anything right!" to "I forgot to take out the trash. Now, how can I do a better job of remembering the trash in the future?"

I have shifted from attacking myself to attacking the problem. That is the healthy response. If someone is watching me carefully, they may catch a little smile crack at the corner of my mouth when I fail. I often think, *Well, well, you have just proved that you are human. Isn't it great!* There is freedom without condemnation, and freedom puts a smile on my face every time.

As I learned to stop the lies of shame and condemnation, I began to experience victory in my thought life. However, there are still times when the lies compound and overwhelm me. One negative thought follows another until I feel like I am mentally spinning out of control. When this happens I am in what John Bradshaw calls a "Shame Spiral." (36) Like their aeronautical counterpart, if I let a shame spiral run its course, it will drive me into the ground! Still, even these can be stopped.

John presents several exercises in his book designed to help stop the shaming thoughts dead in their tracks. The method I found most useful is what John calls "Thought Interruption." [37] I startle myself to interrupt my own train of thought. In a nutshell, the technique is as follows.

1. When I have the first shaming thought that normally results in the shame spiral I shout, "STOP" out loud. The intensity of the shout is equal to the intensity of the emotion associated with the thought.
2. Then I clear my mind of *all* thought for thirty to sixty seconds. The first time I tried this I only managed to keep intruding thoughts out for about five seconds. That was all right. I continue to get better at it.
3. Lastly, I replaced the shaming thought with the truth.

For example, I was washing a glass in the kitchen, and the glass slipped out of my fingers, hit the floor and glass went everywhere. The first thought that crossed my mind was,

You idiot! You can't even ….

"STOP!"

Long pause ….

Wow! That made a mess. It is only a glass, and a glass can be replaced. Now where is that broom and dustpan?

Admittedly, I cannot use this technique while sitting in the middle of a meeting at work. I need to practice in a place of solitude. The good news is that I reached a point where I no longer needed to shout. I only needed to say the word STOP, clear my mind, and then speak the truth. Eventually I did not even need to speak the word out loud. I am now able to form the word in my mind, and it has the same effect as the original shout.

Replacement Thinking

I eventually discovered that it was important not to reinforce the negative, shameful, or general lies in any way. A recurring thought I had when I made a mistake, no matter how minor it was, was, *You are such an idiot*. The truth is that I am not an idiot. I am imperfect, which I now celebrate, but I am not stupid.

When I first attacked these lies, my instinct was to think something along the lines of, *you idiot. You are not stupid!* That did not accomplish a lot; it only reinforced my negative lying thought. This is where replacement thinking came in. Instead of going down the negative path when I identified this lying thought, I tried to simply think, *I am not perfect, but I am smart! This is just a mistake. No more. No less.* What a difference!

The focus is away from what I am not; it is on the truth of what I am.

This is my biggest challenge. There were some areas of my healing that took place in a very short period of time, but this one still remains a challenge. Why did God not provide instant healing? Only He knows for sure, but I suspect it is because He wants me to develop a life-long habit of taking my thoughts captive for Christ. New lies are introduced all of the time, and they need to be dealt with just as ruthlessly as the old ones that have been around since my childhood.

I identified a number of areas in my life where my thought life and the truth did not line up. Thoughts like: *you are an idiot, you cannot do anything right, you will never have a successful relationship, Janet hates you, Janet doesn't know how to have a relationship, she hates men in general, you are only good at work-just accept it,* etc., could go on and on. I love what Janet calls it, "stinkin' thinkin'." Some people find it beneficial to keep a Thought Journal to uncover the areas of "stinkin' thinkin'." I have recommended this to others who have struggled in the same way I did, and at times, do. You simply jot down your self-talk throughout the day. Do not evaluate it. Just record it. At the end of the day, pray through the list, and ask God to start replacing the lies with the truth. When you catch yourself in a self-talk lie, simply pause, replace it with the truth and move on. Then celebrate the truth!

Once I started to pay attention to my thinking, it was so chocked full of recurring lies that it did not take me long to start noticing the pattern. Believe me, that is not a compliment, but it was a reality! One of my many imperfections to celebrate. I am human, after all, and proud of it!

The Truth

Throughout my recovery I put a strong emphasis on the truth. The premise of my life is now based on

...you will know the truth, and the truth will set you free. [38]

Truth revealed itself to be of paramount importance. My freedom was found in it. I had to have a storehouse of truth at my disposal to replace the lies. The best source was, and is, from Truth itself, from God through his Word. It remains vitally important for me to pray and read God's Word each day. To recover, how I read the Bible even had to change. I had to learn to stop reading God's Word through the lens of condemnation. If 1 Corinthians 13 is "the love chapter" then

John 14 is the "comfort chapter." Jesus is about to be crucified and leave his disciples to carry on in His place. They are deeply troubled and He knows it. Because of his great love for His disciples (including me), Jesus said,

> *Do not let your hearts be troubled. Trust in God; trust also in me.*
> (39)

At first I heard condemnation in those words. I believed if my heart was troubled, then I was doing something wrong; I was not trusting in God. I had to pause and read them again. Soon I heard how softly, with love and caring, they were spoken. They are words of comfort. They point to Someone who is greater than my troubled heart. Someone who can bring comfort. I read it again, reveling in God's kind voice. Jesus goes on to say,

> *In my Father's house are many rooms; if it were not so, I would have told you. I am going there to prepare a place for you. And if I go and prepare a place for you, I will come back and take you to be with me that you also may be where I am.* (40)

This truly was my comfort chapter. I can feel the very heartbeat of God and His love toward me. I am not someone He just tolerates, which was my previous mindset. He truly loves me and wants to be with *me*. Later on in this chapter Jesus says,

> *Whoever has my commands and obeys them, he is the one who loves me. He who loves me will be loved by my Father, and I, too, will love him and show myself to him.* (41)

In the past I experienced instant condemnation when I read this verse! I would think to myself, *Sometimes I do not obey Jesus. In fact, sometimes I knowingly go directly against what I know He wants. I do not really love Jesus. I may not even be saved!*

My misinterpretation of scripture came through my filter of self-condemnation. Jesus was not asking the disciples to be perfect. Peter himself denied Jesus just a short time later. Jesus was acknowledging their obedience, that was their heart, and their actions matched their hearts much of the time. He was confirming His love for them and the Father's love as well.

I know that because

> There is now no condemnation for those who are in Christ Jesus. (42)

How much is "no"? It is none. Nada. Zilch. Zip. Not a fraction of condemnation. Jesus was encouraging them with the reality that they were loved by Him and His Father. Is there any greater source of comfort and encouragement in life? Not for me!

Right Thinking

Fully equipped to attack my "stinkin' thinkin'," I searched for a new place for my thoughts to go. God gave me some good, solid direction here as well.

> Finally, brothers, whatever is true, whatever is noble, whatever is right, whatever is pure, whatever is lovely, whatever is admirable—if anything is excellent or praiseworthy—think about such things. (43)

This was my new grid for my thought life. Take my thoughts captive. Determine if they are true. Believe them if they are, and discard them if they are not. Noble thinking called me to a higher place. I choose to embrace it. Pure? I get to just enjoy it. Lovely? I now enjoy its beauty. Is it worth admiring? Is it excellent? Praiseworthy? If so, then this is something worth thinking about. Right thinking uplifts my spirit and puts a smile on my face in spite of the circumstances. "Stinkin' thinkin'" just drags me down.

Guilt vs. Shame

I am not advocating guilt-free living. There is a place for properly placed responsibility. The feeling that I get when I have genuinely done something wrong is very different than the shame that I have experienced for many years. Whether I call it guilt or healthy shame, it all points to the same thing. Responsibility. How can I tell the difference?

Shame attacks the person (me). Guilt attacks the problem.

If my thinking takes me down the "I am" path of condemnation, then in all likelihood, it is shame. I have also noticed that condemnation does not like to be alone; it seeks out its friends. One condemning thought leads to another. It does not take long for my attitude about everything and everyone to become soured.

If the thought takes me on the "I did" path, then it is probably guilt. When it is guilt I take responsibility because it is something I have done. The way I had hurt my wife over the years is my responsibility. Since it is something that I did, not who I am, I could change. This is one more truth that leads to freedom.

What About My Thoughts of Her?

While we are on the subject of changing my thoughts, I will go ahead and tackle a delicate subject. How did I handle the way I thought about Janet? The truth is I had a boatload of lies that I had believed about my wife. It was time to start over.

I no longer spend much time or energy thinking about Janet's *issues*. I had focused on how Janet was wrong for many years. Today I try to stay focused on how she is right. I needed to stay focused on the truth as God revealed it to me over the weeks and months. With healing came adult eyes and a changed perspective of Janet. The truth is that she is an amazing, steadfast, kind, patient, loving woman who hung on for many years in a marriage that was unbearable. She absolutely deserves a medal!

Is It a Wrap?

This does not mean that I never have a negative thought. When a driver comes barging into my lane, I will likely, and appropriately, have a negative reaction. First, I get out of his or her way! Then I take my thoughts captive, moving from reactive (yelling at the top of my lungs, "You are such an idiot!" and possible inappropriate hand gesture to the other driver) to active (*That was a close one. Lord, thank you for protecting us both*). This is the path I want to be on.

I never could have taken this journey alone. Because of the depth of my wounds, I needed a trusted friend and a counselor to walk with me through the healing process. If I could have solved this on my own, I would have probably done it by now. I had to learn to reach out for help from others. I am so glad that I did.

The Road to Assertiveness

Assertiveness is a behavior and skill that helped me to communicate, clearly and with confidence, my feelings, needs, wants and thoughts...at the same time valuing others and respecting their right to an opinion as well. [44]

There are two paths that lead to attempts to control and manipulate others. They are attempts to control a world that feels out of control and appears to threaten our very existence. They are the choices of passive-aggressive and aggressive behavior. Striking someone is aggressive. Yelling, screaming and intimidating to get your way, is aggressive behavior. Even a glance that says, "Don't even try it..." is aggressive behavior.

Passive-aggressive behavior is much harder to identify. It is one of the reasons that Janet and I had such a hard time finding help. It is harder to identify things that are missing than finding things that do not belong.

The chart below shows the differences between passive, assertive and aggressive behaviors. It helped me choose to live my life in the center column.

Passive (Non-Assertive)	Assertive	Aggressive
Problems are avoided	**The problem is attacked**	The person is attacked
Legitimate rights are stuffed	**Legitimate rights are claimed**	Your rights are claimed
Rights of others are viewed as superior to yours	**Rights of others are seen as equal to yours**	You view your rights as superior to others' rights
Establishes patterns of others taking advantage of you	**Establishes a pattern of respect for future dealings**	Establishes patterns of fear and avoidance of the aggressor
Lets the other person guess how you think and feel	**Lets the other person know how you think and feel**	Lets the other person know how you think [no communication of

Passive (Non-Assertive)	Assertive	Aggressive
		feeling]
Hopes goals may be achieved	**Works toward goals**	Works toward goals using force
Lets others choose activities for you	**Chooses activities for self**	Chooses your own activities and the activities of others
Builds anger and resentment	**Deals properly with anger**	Acts out of anger
Talks to others with respect for others, not yourself	**Talks to others with respect for the person and for self**	Talks down to others
Lacks confidence	**Confident**	Cocky and hostile
Hopes for favors and services (but never asks)	**Requests favors and services**	Demands favors and services

Characteristics of passive, assertive and aggressive problem solving
Paul Hegstrom and Life Skills International, Inc. [45]

Conquering my passive-aggressive behavior was not possible through the exercise of my raw will. That approach only left me exhausted. The secret to conquering both passive-aggressive and aggressive behavior is the same as it is for shame; I put on my lie detector, but instead of taking my thoughts captive, I took my reactions prisoner, moving from a reactive to an active lifestyle.

For example, one of the roles I played was that of martyr. Let's say I have ridden a long bike ride on Saturday morning, and I have come home and cut the grass to get ready for a party later that evening. Janet has been gone all morning and does not know what I have done. She is busy with making preparations and notices that we are out of hamburger buns.

Janet asks, "Greg, will you please run to the store and get us some whole wheat hamburger buns?"

The martyr: Long sigh, "Sure honey, I will go in just a minute..." I feel a twinge of resentment, but I push it away before I even recognize what I am experiencing because it is "wrong." I plough through in spite of being exhausted. I think to myself, *I am going to be worthless at this party tonight...* I am short-tempered with Janet later that evening, and I do not even know why. The resentment is there, but I do not allow it to surface.

Assertive: "Sweetheart, I am really tired right now. I'm going to rest a while, maybe close my eyes for a few minutes, then go. Will that work?" She agrees, I get some rest, get the buns, and we have a great time together at the party.

Both responses achieve the same result; I still go to get the hamburger buns. In the first response I stuffed my legitimate right to rest (passive), which led to resentment. In the second response I was assertive, voiced my real need for rest, and it was accommodated.

In order for this to work, I needed to be honest about my legitimate needs, wants and especially my feelings. This meant experiencing the full human range of emotions and understanding when they were at work. Of course, to do that I needed to feel again.

Feeling Again

Emotions were created by God. They are meant to serve us. In ways, I think the American Christian church has done us a disservice in the lack of teaching around emotions. In many churches there is a silent rule; we are only allowed to have one emotion, and that is joy. If we are not joyful, something is wrong with us, so it is time to fake it until we make it! Since it is not natural, or healthy, to have such a limited range of emotion, we never make it; we just fake it!

I had buried my pain so far deep down inside that my emotions did not even come along for the ride. Janet's description of me as an "emotional flat liner" was not far from the truth. This is an area where I was completely unable to make even a start on my own. Enter John, my psychologist and counselor.

The first time I visited John's office was about three months after Gene's visit. When Gene left I spent two months working through shame with a combination of prayer, reading and Theophostics. I sensed my progress was slowing, and so did Janet. I went in search of someone who could help me get moving again. The search turned out to be more difficult than I imagined. Here is a typical conversation with a counselor's office.

"Hello, my name is Greg Tilford. I am wondering if <fill in the name> is familiar with Arrested Emotional Development and its treatment."

"Will you please hold?"

"Of course."

A short time passes.

"<name> does both individual and couple counseling."

"Yes, but does <name> have specific experience with Arrested Emotional Development?"

"Will you hold please?"

"Yes."

Another short time passes.

"<name> is not specifically familiar with that term, but <name> will be happy to see you. Do you want to make an appointment?"

"No. Thank you for your time." Click.

I do not remember how many offices I called, or how many Internet searches I performed, but it was more than I like to think about. I was desperate for help, but it was nowhere to be found. After a few weeks of off-and-on searching through the Internet in the Dallas area, I had a hit on AED! I was excited and called the office immediately.

"Hello, my name is Greg Tilford. I am wondering if John is familiar with Arrested Emotional Development and its treatment."

"Yes, John treats Arrested Emotional Development in both teens and adults. Do you want to make an appointment?"

"Yes!"

Score! There was once again hope.

My First Meeting - RAD

At my first session John asked why I had come. After all the phone calls and trying to find a counselor who could help, I had my thoughts down to an elevator speech. I described the issues that Janet and I had encountered in our marriage and in life in general. I also reviewed all that Gene had shown me about AED. Of course, John had his own set of questions, and by the end of the session, he was ready to give his initial first impression.

John said that AED was a fairly broad term. Indications were that my problem was specifically Reactive Attachment Disorder, or RAD. There was only one problem. RAD is typically diagnosed in children and young adults, not full grown men! Nevertheless, it fit.

If caregivers are not reliably or consistently present or if they respond in an unpredictable and uncertain way, babies are not able to establish a pattern of confident expectation. One result is insecure attachment, or a less-than-optimal internal sense of confidence and trust in others, beginning with caregivers. The child then uses psychological defenses (e.g., avoidance or ambivalence) to avoid disappointments with the caregiver. This is thought to contribute to a negative working model of relationships that leads to insecurity for the rest of the child's life. [46]

I fit into the "rest of the child's life" sentence well. It described my "mommy" issues to a tee. I asked John, "What is the solution?" I fully expected a detailed treatment plan.

Instead John answered, "It is simple. Janet is Janet. Mom is Mom."

I was stunned. What? Could it be that simple?

It was that simple … to say; it was not that simple to do. I had projected childhood needs onto Janet that she never could nor should meet. Janet and Mom seemed hopelessly enmeshed. It took time to pick the two apart. I kept the constant mantra on my mind. *Janet is Janet, Mom is Mom!* When I felt like Janet was correcting me, which impressed me as a very motherly activity, I repeated my mantra. Anytime a negative thought crossed my mind about Janet, I silently repeated, *Janet is Janet, Mom is Mom…* I was slowly rewiring my brain.

But I had another significant issue. I did not feel.

Biofeedback

I described earlier how I drove the meter off the scale in my first biofeedback session with John when he asked the simple question, "Tell me about your mother." In the weeks and months ahead, biofeedback became my frequent friend. Why was it so important? Because I did not know when I felt something. I buried my feelings so deep that I blew right through an emotion without noticing a single twinge or tingle. The emotions were there, or the biofeedback would not have registered. Somehow I managed to severely deaden the emotional link between my conscious and subconscious mind, so I did not experience the full pain of my past. Unfortunately, this also meant that I only experienced a very limited range of the pain or joys of the present. It was as if I performed a self-lobotomy. No real highs, no real lows. But it was all a self-deception. The emotions were there. They did affect me. I lived exhausted every moment of every day. I was dragging my past with me like a ball and chain, and it was destroying my future.

Biofeedback was the tool that John used to give him the clue that he needed to probe a little deeper. He could tell when I was lying to myself. The meter betrayed me every time, and I welcomed its betrayal. It also started to help me connect my emotions to events again.

When John would say, "What was that?" it was my clue to ask myself, *what did you just feel*? At first the answer was, *absolutely nothing*! Over time my emotions started to surface to a conscious level, little by little.

It was strange at first. I had to give myself permission to feel. My enemies, my emotions, were becoming my friends. I had to walk through long-buried pain. "The way out is through" was still ringing true. But it was not all sackcloth and ashes. Something else started to happen. I started to *feel* joy. I did not need to plaster a smile on my face because that is how I was supposed to feel. I started to actually, in all its wonderful, tingly ways, experience joy in little things in life. I started to wake up every morning happy. I had never experienced that before in my life. My whole life I started each day with a sense of dread. Now I was experiencing something foreign, yet wonderful. Joy! What a bonus!

It's Time to Stop Feeling Less Than

Janet is a smart, attractive, assertive and capable woman. I always recognized this, but I assumed that as I moved through my healing process that the perceived gap between us would dramatically shrink. It did not! Although I had a growing sense of my own value and capabilities, the more I looked at Janet, my perceptions of her as a woman only grew. It turned out that she is smarter, more attractive, more assertive and an even more capable woman than I ever knew! I felt undone!

The answer came one Sunday in church. I was minding my own business in worship when I had another one of those Holy Spirit moments when God spoke to my spirit.

It is time to stop feeling less than.

I immediately knew what He meant. I broke down and started to cry. I felt "less than" my entire life. Everyone else appeared more capable than I; they were the adults, I was the child. That "less than" was grounded in a lie. The "less than" that I was experiencing now was grounded in truth! There are people, many of them in fact, who are smarter than I. There are many people more confident than I. There are men better looking than I. The "more than I" list seemed like it was almost infinite.

Now that I was seeing myself with adult eyes, flaws and all, what was I to do? The solution was simple. Stop comparing. Stop feeling less than. I had to learn to be content being exactly who God created me to be and stop making comparisons to others. Every person God created is unique.

For you created my inmost being; you knit me together in my mother's womb. I praise you because I am fearfully and wonderfully made; your works are wonderful, I know that full well. My frame was not hidden from you when I was made in the secret place. When I was woven together in the depths of the earth, your eyes saw my unformed body. All the days ordained for me were written in your book before one of them came to be. (47)

I am purpose built. I was built by God for His purpose. I am no accident. I was not an unplanned, unwanted pregnancy to God. I came on the scene exactly when he wanted me to. (48) And he has great things for me that He prepared in eternity past. (49) I am a work in progress, but more and more every day, I feel like I belong exactly where I find myself. It is exactly where God wants me to be. This gives me the confidence to be authentic and to like myself just exactly the way I am. This puts a smile on my face. When I look in the mirror, I like the person who smiles back at me.

Theo-what's It?

Another important tool that God used in my healing process was Theophostics.

> *Theo (God) Phostic (light) is a ministry of prayer that is Christ-centered and God-reliant for its direction and outcome. Simply stated, it is encouraging a person to discover and expose what he believes is a falsehood; and then encouraging him to have an encounter with Jesus Christ through prayer, thus allowing the Lord to reveal His truth to the wounded person's heart and mind. … It is about allowing a person to have a personal encounter with the Lord Jesus in the midst of the person's emotional pain.* (50)

It is simple, but in practice the dynamics are amazing. Some dear friends, Terry and Patti, are well-trained in Theophostic Prayer Ministry and have helped many people find freedom from issues that have plagued them for years. I had an "issue" that I just could not get around, my perceptions of my mother.

In Theophostics you start with the earliest memory you have of an often painful situation. When I closed my eyes I saw my mother standing in the kitchen. I felt absolutely alone even though she was in the same room with me. It felt like we occupied the same space but not the same life. I saw the black and white checkered linoleum floor, the door to the porch off the back of the kitchen, and the dark Formica topped table. My mother was there just sitting at the table and smoking a cigarette, but she was not engaged with me in any way. I wanted her to love and appreciate me. I wanted her to be proud of me, to at least acknowledge my existence. Instead, there was no connection, and all that I felt was sadness.

Then something strange began to happen. My intention was to experience her as a child and to start to work through the painful emotions of abandonment when the next thing that I knew I was a man standing next to her in my mind's eye!

It was as if I were looking in on a moment of my past as an uninvolved observer. I saw the lines of worry and sadness on her face. She stared off into the distance as she was exploring some unknown pain of her own, slowly puffing on a cigarette as she often did. I saw her through adult eyes, and I felt compassion toward *her* pain, for *her* loneliness. Even now as I write this paragraph, it brings tears to my eyes. It is doubtful that I will ever know the source of that pain, but I knew, for the very first time, that it did not have anything to do with me. Instead of Jesus coming and comforting me, I received comfort from the certain knowledge that her disinterest in me was not my fault.

I turned an important corner that day. I moved from, "It is my mother's fault that I have the issues in my life" to the realization that she carried her own pain. She loved me the best she could. She cared for me the best she could. It may not have been enough, but the pain she inflicted was not malicious. It was simply the outworking of her pain. I moved from hurt and resentment toward my mother to compassion that day.

Does My Wife Have a Part?

Where is Janet's part in all of this? For twenty-nine years I focused on Janet…if she would just accept me…if she would be more loving…if she would be less judgmental…the theme went on and on and on. The truth is that there is only one person responsible for my thoughts, attitudes, and behavior.

That person is I. Once I fully accepted this truth, I was ready for the next part of my journey.

The chances of Janet having issues of her own were very strong. Like attracts like. Janet and I were attracted to each other in healthy ways, but we also had areas of unhealthy attraction. Otherwise, she would have never entered into a relationship with someone with "mommy" issues like mine. She knew my flaws and married me anyway.

This thinking is where the danger lies. There is no place for "I knew it!" in my thoughts because that only takes the focus off me. Janet's issues are hers and hers alone. I can support her in change, but I cannot prod, manipulate or motivate her to change. I am not her Holy Spirit, and I have enough on my plate with just me!

One counselor asked her why it took so long for her to say "no more!" Janet had two responses. First, she did not know what "It" was. Trying to describe my behavior was a lot like trying to nail Jell-O to a wall. I was loving/unloving, kind/unkind, and supportive/distant all at the same time. To say that this was confusing to Janet is an understatement. Second, she believed that she and Jesus could make it through anything.

What finally changed for her was that God told her to leave. She argued with Him, believing that what He was asking of her was very un-God-like. She said, "You and I can do anything!" He then told her that,

Yes, we can do anything and right now, we are going to leave.

My primary issue was rooted in Mom and Janet being one and the same to me. Every moment with Janet took me a step away from my healing. I had to stare abandonment square in the face and survive. I believed abandonment was worse than death. Janet's leaving broke that lie once and for all.

Her leaving also took away all desire for band-aid fixes. It quickly became about total, complete, full inner healing *for me*. I am glad God knew what He was doing because neither of us had a clue. He never promised Janet that her leaving would break the final front of resistance to my healing. He never told her that it would all work out in the end. Just as God told Abraham to *leave your country, your people and your father's household and go to the land I will show you,* [51] God asked Janet to leave all that was familiar to set out to wherever He decided to lead. It took faith. It took courage.

Coming Together Again

Janet and I both had our ideas about how it would look to end our separation and re-join together as truly husband and wife. The day it happened was totally different than either of us ever imagined. After Janet cancelled the divorce, and I started to make some progress, we met over a six-month period for an occasional coffee or to share a lunch at the house. Three months after I began to work with John, Janet stopped by the house to drop something off, and we began talking. Suddenly, out of the blue, she asked if she could come home.

Janet says that she had spent the last month looking deeply into possible solutions if she came home and six months later everything fell apart. She had come up with the outlandish solution of giving me food that I was allergic to. I would then behave like a crazy man, and she would have the police haul me away!

Her friends, Chris and Robin, ministered to her for hours. The Lord showed her that with good friends and church support, she would be able to make it should it all fall apart again. Her escape would be through God, not through her own clever plans. Chris and Robin believed for the best for us, and that God would get her through. This was very important for her after living with twenty-nine years of abuse. She knew exactly what failure would look and feel like.

Suddenly, sitting with me in our home that Friday afternoon in June, she felt the Lord's permission come over her. I said yes as soon as she asked about coming home.

God was at work in me as well, and I was coming to the end of my rope with the separation. It was starting to feel unnecessary and forced, like there really was no reason for us to be separated any longer. In ways it was strange and foreign to me; I no longer *needed* Janet. If she had told me that day that she wanted to end the marriage, no discussions, period, end of story, for the first time in my life I knew I would be fine. My life would not end. It would not be the end of the world. I would be saddened, but I certainly would not have blamed Janet. I had sown so much pain into her life that I would have been reaping what I had sown.

The real miracle is, although I did not need Janet, I wanted her. I wanted her companionship. I wanted her smile in our home again. Although I knew that I was not completely on the other side of my healing, I believed we would be better together than apart. It was time for us to be what a husband and wife are supposed to be to each other, a safe place for the other where love and support flourish and grow. It was time for our marriage not to merely survive, but to grow and thrive!

We did not just go from separation to voila, fantastic marriage! After doing the necessary work, we were new and that was exciting. No old dead marriage to contend with and no old dead relationship either. Pain and disappointment were now replaced with love and respect.

Taking the Risk, Again ...

Even with all the wonderful possibilities, I knew that there would be some skepticism on Janet's part, and she had every right to it. I had no grounds to demand anything from her, not even reconciliation. I was the main source of our marital failure. My actions throughout the marriage had taken a toll. I had destroyed the trust in our marriage with my version of Dr. Jekyll and Mr. Hyde. She fell in love with Dr. Jekyll. Unless she truly believed that Mr. Hyde was long gone, she would not want to risk the pain from him again. She had every right to be cautious.

I was very fortunate that Janet wanted our reconciliation to work. I did not need to convince her of the value of our family being together again. So, with a little apprehension, but with a lot of excitement, we started to re-engage.

The Guiding Principles

For us to come together again as husband and wife, I had to follow three guiding principles. The first was for me to remain focused on my goals for wholeness. Period. The main focus could not be on reconciliation or the reunification of my marriage with Janet. Even during the time of reconciliation, everything else took a back seat to my healing progress.

The second principle is equally as simple. I had to know that I would fail and to know that it was an opportunity to further the first principle, my healing. When I noticed something pushing my buttons, I quickly moved from reaction to responding and asked myself, *Why did that bother me? What is going on inside of me that I need to deal with*? It is never, ever, ever about Janet, no matter what she said or did. Ever! Why? Because I cannot control another individual; I can only control me.

I found myself, at times, in situations from which I needed to remove myself because I had not received the level of healing needed to handle the situation. Unfortunately, Janet and I did not have any agreement on how to handle these situations when we were coming back together. There were times when Janet hit a major nerve, and I used my old coping mechanism and went into emotional shut down. She would see my eyes go distant, and it would trigger fear in her. It was an old cycle that played itself out for months before I learned to stay engaged, even when my emotions triggered painful memories. It would have been much simpler and more productive for me to have been honest with her and let her know what was going on inside of me, but I was still using the old habit of pushing through instead of allowing myself to be vulnerable.

Now we have agreed that either of us can break off a conversation or activity without explanation if we feel things starting to spin out of control. This is not to be used as a mechanism for control or avoidance. If I break something off, we mutually agree on a day and time when I will re-engage. She has the same opportunity to process her feelings before we attempt to work through the issue.

The third principle was, take it slow. How slow? As slowly as we needed for both of us to be comfortable with each other in a wide range of situations. We used the times that we got together for lunch and coffee dates for our own purposes. It looked a lot like courting - a time to get to know each other.

Starting Fresh

Previously we both agreed that the relationship that we had had did not simply need to change, it needed to die. It was as if Janet was meeting me for the first time. She never really knew the real Greg. She had glimpses, but after all, how could she know what was real? I said "Yes" when I felt "No!" Many of my emotions were faked since I rarely experienced anything real. What was real?

On my side I was relating to Janet for the first time as my wife and not my mother. All of the dynamics were different. Our relationship needed a fresh start.

No Rush for the Physical

We learned from Gene that intimate relationships progress in definite steps. If sex is brought into the relationship too soon, it short-circuits the process, and it can prevent a relationship from reaching its full potential. Sex can become a substitute for true, growing intimacy. The Arrested Emotional Development guaranteed that my relationships never fully matured. Now we had the opportunity to do it right and create a loving, growing relationship from a place of wholeness and respect.

The next chart [52] illustrates these key steps that our relationship went through as we grew closer together.

BUILDING A RELATIONSHIP
(Normalcy is to go through each of the 13 steps)

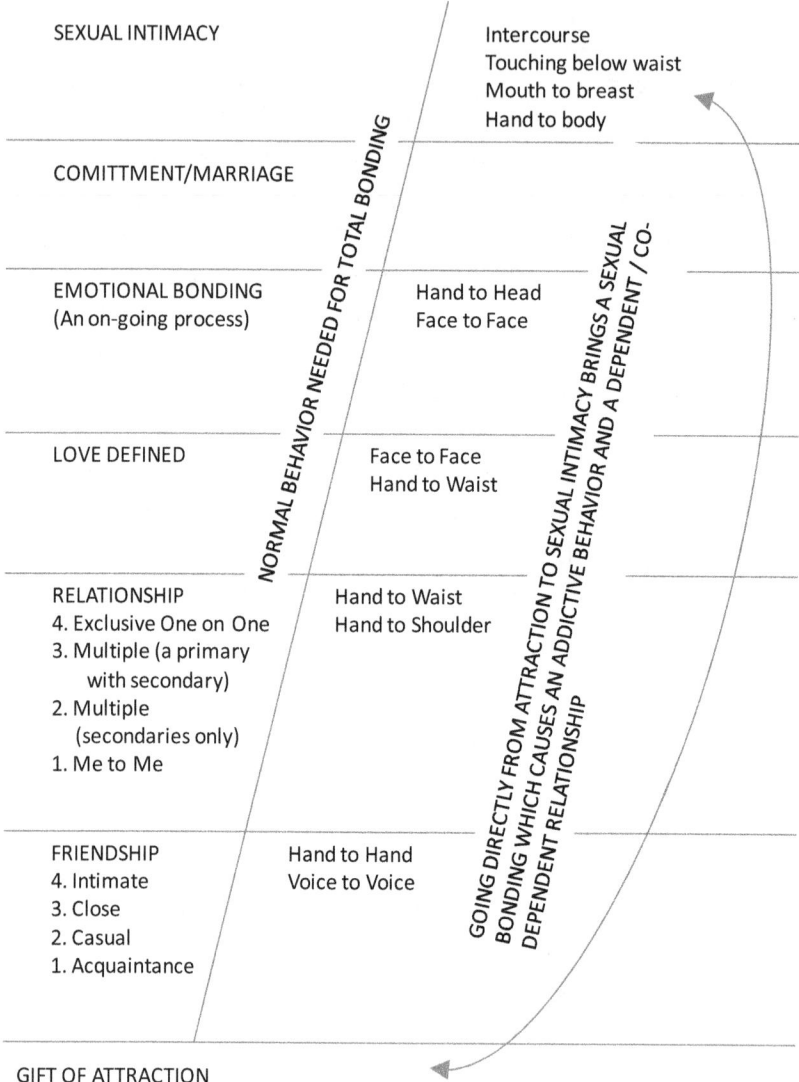

Paul Hegstrom and Life Skills International, Inc.

The chart moves from the bottom to the top. There is no hope for sexual intimacy preceding friendship in a healthy relationship. The fact that we both were willing to try to reconcile indicates that there was still attraction. That was great for us! We had a starting point. After attraction we needed to develop our friendship afresh.

Friendship

As in all friendships there are different levels. We started out as acquaintances and moved to a more intimate[4] friendship in both the depth of our conversations and range of topics and interests that we pursued together. Janet and I would meet at a coffee shop from time to time to talk, or Janet would come over to the house to have lunch. Initially our time together was limited to about an hour.

At this stage of the relationship, I limited my physical contact with Janet to what I would do with someone's ninety-year-old grandmother. If I gave her a hug, it was with great care!

Relationship

After friendship came relationship. Relationships have the connotation of exclusivity. Janet and I both continued to behave as if we were married even after the separation, so moving into an exclusive relationship was not an issue for us. We experienced this transition in our relationship when we both knew that reconciliation was a real possibility. I was starting to believe that our family could come back together again.

---

[4]Intimacy and sex are not the same thing. It is possible to have deep intimacy without sex, and you can have sex without intimacy. When I speak of intimacy, I am talking about a relationship where souls truly touch.

I told Janet that I was not willing for our relationship to merely survive; it would thrive! I continued to pursue my healing. This was where it felt like Janet really started to push my buttons. The truth was that she was just being herself. Like open wounds, the slightest touch caused pain. I had many conversations with my counselor, John, during this period. Our interaction uncovered a number of areas where I still needed both healing and understanding.

Our physical relationship during this stage remained that of brother and sister. This ensured that we continued to grow closer emotionally without the complications of a sexual relationship.

Love Defined and Emotional Bonding

As I began to relate to Janet man to woman, I started to experience the emotion of love toward her in ways that I had never experienced before. It bothered me when someone emotionally hurt her. I prayed for her personal breakthroughs without the comparisons and feelings of inadequacy that I experienced before. I was truly becoming her man, and she, my woman. She started feeling protected by me. This is something that she had never experienced before. In the past I deflected blame to Janet so I would not experience the shame of my own failures. As I stayed connected to her, as I listened to her, and even bore the burden of the knowledge of how I hurt her, our bonding deepened. I was, for the first time, truly man enough to take it. She was beginning to trust me again. Unknown to Janet, I was starting to trust her for the first time. Even if our relationship did not make it all the way, my respect and admiration for Janet was growing.

According to "the chart" it was perfectly legitimate to start experiencing some level of physical intimacy, like kissing, at this point in our relationship. However, I decided early in our reconciliation process that I did not want to do anything to hamper the progress of our emotional bonding. I had a good example to follow in this area… our oldest son, Brett.

Our son and his wife both had their first kiss at the altar the day of their marriage. They not only committed to remain sexually pure before marriage, but Maggie wanted their wedding to be the first time they experienced the kind of physical intimacy you experience through a kiss. They have an incredibly strong and growing marriage today, and I think their decision to delay physical intimacy played a vital role in growing an emotionally intimate relationship first.

Intimacy, according to Gene is:

Being vulnerable to another human being.

Intimacy is about letting down your guard and letting another human being get so close that you share both the pains and joys of life. In my life of AED, sex was equal to intimacy. In fact, it was the only place where I lowered my guard enough to experience any intimacy at all. However, seven-year-old children do not know how to be intimate, so it was something I had never truly experienced in an emotionally mature way. I was committed to learning how to have an intimate relationship with Janet without sex!

Commitment/Marriage & Sexual Intimacy

We never had any intimate physical contact, kissing or otherwise, until the night that we mutually decided that it was time for Janet to come home. Janet had tested and tried me enough that she was willing to risk being together again. And it was a risk. She worked through enough of her healing to stay strong during my relapses. Two times she had to fall back on Chris and Robin for emotional support and clarity. It made all the difference for her to have good friends that were safe, encouraging and supportive. They were able to believe despite all of our humanity.

I was willing to take the risk of being hurt again. Even if Janet left, it was not abandonment. It would be Janet, an adult, making a decision of what was necessary for her to not just survive in life, but thrive.

I never experienced love making like I did that night. I thought I would be nervous. It was over a year since we had been together sexually, but that night there were no masks and no agendas. Janet was just expressing her love toward me, and I, my love toward her. We slept peacefully next to each other all night. Although we had had a honeymoon thirty years before, that was the first night of true sweetness that I had ever experienced.

From the time I was seven, through my early teen years, and all the years of our marriage, my sex drive had been insatiable. Once we reunited my sex drive was dramatically lower. Was something wrong with me? Did those months of deprivation do some permanent damage? Nothing is further from the truth. I was experiencing intimacy in so many other non-sexual ways with Janet that I was emotionally satisfied for the first time in my life.

Prior to my healing I was like a parched man in the desert, getting his thirst quenched one drop at a time. Each sexual encounter only provided a single drop of intimacy, and I was dying of relational thirst! After God healed me emotionally, it was like drinking from a fire hose. It was so easy to get my fill! Janet and I experience that kind of intimacy today when we make love or when we sit down eye-to-eye, heart-to-heart, and share a cup of coffee. Intimacy is so much more than sex. It is life-giving. It is essential. It is being vulnerable with another person, and the primary person for me is Janet. If necessary I can live without sex but not without intimacy.

Janet and I had achieved our initial goal. We reached a point where we were better together than apart.

Dealing with Habits

As good as things were, both Janet and I were completely caught off guard by old habits creeping into our new relationship.

Even though we had leaned into God, been honest with our therapist/coach and we had each received the inner healing we needed to have an emotionally healthy relationship, we still had behavioral habits that we needed to break.

We stayed honest and alert. Since I now *felt* my emotions, I had to pay attention to them. If I got a niggling feeling that something was not right, I learned that something was not right! I began to trust my feelings. If I failed, I admitted it immediately to my Janet. It still is not unusual for me to say to Janet, "You know, what I just told you is not true at all. I am still learning to …." Janet normally graciously understands, and we work through the issue.

For example, although I no longer feel a wave of panic when Janet and I disagree, I am still prone to argue. It was my *modus operandi* for many years. I will catch myself, or Janet will catch me, and I have to check my motives on the spot. Do I believe I am right? How important is it to be right? Am I arguing instead of just listening? Am I arguing over details, or am I objecting to the heart of the conversation?

All of these thoughts, and more, will flash through my mind. In most cases I am answering before hearing Janet's heart, and I check my objections. It is not unusual to find that once the conversation plays itself out we are in complete agreement. Janet likes to say, "We may come in through different doors, but we often find ourselves standing in the same room." In fact, we agree now far more than we disagree.

Some other habits that I had to deal with were my reactions around discussing finances, the tension around holidays, bad days (we all have them), sick days, relearning sex (from action to intimacy), and more. I had to beware of habits and not allow fear to creep into my relationship. If I have a recurring problem that I cannot resolve, I seek outside help. The key is that we stay united, attacking the problem, not each other. Those days are over. We have a new relationship.

By this time we were experiencing another major miracle in our relationship. We did not need to *try* to make things work. We were experiencing *effortless effort*. This strange term describes perfectly how our relationship was working. Yes, it took some effort, but it was more like the effort of an ice skater gliding across the rink than a mountain climber going up a sheer rock face! It only took a little push in the right direction, and the momentum felt right and exhilarating. We have heard people say that marriage is hard work. We agreed with them for years. Now, we totally and completely disagree. We did hard...*this* is not hard! *This* is fun, refreshing, lifegiving and amazing! Today our marriage is starting to truly reflect the relationship of Jesus, the Bridegroom, and the Church, His Bride. It is life-giving.

Facing Consequences

Has it been all waterfalls, grassy glens and roses since we have reunited? Of course not! We both sensed that it was time to be a team working through issues *together*.

When Janet and I first got back together, one of the hardest things for me to hear was how I had hurt her over the years. I wanted the past to be erased, and I really did not want to talk about it…at all. This was both selfish and unrealistic. I can still remember sitting in my truck under a tree in our backyard where Janet told me, "It happened. It's real and I'm home. If it's not real, then I'm leaving. You are a strong man, and you can handle what you have done."

Was I? Could I? I went silent and started to listen. Janet poured her heart out to how I had hurt her and how she was still living the consequences of my behavior in her life today. This never occurred to me. It was as if someone turned on a light in a previously dark room, and I saw the contents of the room for the first time. This room was filled with consequences.

One big consequence is that, for a season, we lost nearly every friend we ever had. Part of this I can understand. Since I was absolutely, totally and completely convinced that the majority of my problems in life were because of Janet, I had absolutely, totally and completely convinced others of the same thing. My complete "about face" from blaming Janet to blaming myself was both confusing and disquieting. Some thought I had "sold out" just to get us back under the same roof. Others did not know what to think, so they avoided us all together.

Second, our very presence as a happy, growing couple brings conviction about the nagging problems in their own marriages. It took us both a while to catch on to this dynamic.

There were a number of godly women, who are leaders in several churches, who appealed to Janet with essentially the same story.

They told her, "Every wife will tell you that their husband is a child at times. Their male ego is very fragile. You just build them up. A good wife builds up her husband with respect and adoration."

We once heard a pastor tell his congregation, "Wives, your husband had intact self-esteems before you got a hold of them. You have torn them down for years, and they have no self-esteem left. You need to know that there are a hundred women out there who will show your husband respect. This is his number one need, to be respected."

A few even said, "We've lived separately as brother and sister for ten years. But God hates divorce, and we are not going to do it!"

The final sentence is the most shocking. Without knowing it they were saying that God cared more about them maintaining the façade of marriage than having a truly life-giving marriage. This upside-down thinking is pervasive in the churches today. It has been sold well, and scores of congregations have bought it. We are living proof that it is a lie. God loved us both too much to leave us in the darkness. Janet sought answers for many years, and she found them. When I finally got to the end of myself, God was there to meet me and restore me as well.

Another consequence is that our finances are not as solid as they should be at this stage of life. I was afraid to aggressively invest money because I might lose it. I also said "yes" to a business that I believed was a bad investment, but I did not speak up because I was afraid of the emotional response from

Janet. This was a complete lie. When I finally admitted the truth to Janet, she told me that she was looking for honest input, and we could have avoided the whole disaster if I was truthful.

Although there is a litany of other consequences, one deserves special attention. It remains my greatest burden. How have I affected the next generation, my adult children?

Healing for the Next Generation

All negative behaviors have negative consequences. There are times when God graciously protects the next generation from our mistakes. Other times He allows them to pass through. Unfortunately my behavior affected more than just my wife. It affected my children as well. I asked my youngest son, Josh, to describe his life while he was growing up in our family. Since he is our youngest son, Josh directly experienced both the time when I was stuck in AED, and the time God was leading me through the process of recovery. His impressions tell a familiar story.

I have always wanted to love my dad deeply. However, through much of my life, this was not the reality of our relationship. I could not get comfortable around him. I sensed deep frustration in his life.

I have a gap in my memory of times with my dad. The early years were golden. From the time I was three to around seven years old, I looked up to my dad and loved spending time with him. When I was just three years old, he bought my brother and me BB guns. He taught us how to load the "bullets" as I saw them, shoulder the stock, sight before shooting, and all of the safety precautions involved- two of which I will never forget: I was not allowed to shoot at metal or people and was to keep the safety on until I was ready to fire. These small lessons are what shape boys into grown men, and I could not have gotten enough of it. My dad was my hero, and I wanted to be like him.

I began swimming during the summers with the City of Allen Swim Team when I was four years old and loved it. This led to more competitive swimming that I started around eight years old. That's when my memories of quality time with my dad slim down to just a few here and there. It wasn't that we didn't spend time together. He would go to most of my swim meets, pick me up from practice regularly, and help me with my math homework (for which I am eternally grateful). However, that irreplaceable father-son connection all but disappeared. I sensed tension in his life, and it kept me from being able to relax in his presence. My perception of him was a man who would consistently get angry about little things like being late, not being able to find the keys, etc., and who only fully relaxed when he would call it a night, earlier than the rest of my family, and was by himself in my parents' bedroom, reading.

Josh's perceptions are dead on. As he grew older I began to feel more and more inadequate as a father. I "checked out." I abandoned as I had been abandoned. I was unwittingly ensuring that the history of abandonment would repeat itself in the next generation. Josh continues:

I could never put a finger on it nor understand my dad. I figured it was just the way he was: an introverted, engineering personality. Unlike when I would hang out with my mom, I never felt comfortable around my dad, enough to relax and to be myself. I felt pressure to be productive and to perform.

The generation influenced by AED does not necessarily have the same drivers as the first generation. Josh was never sexually molested. He had a loving and involved mother.

However, he did live in a household with a member who had AED (me), and so he lived with my responses and was influenced by my lifestyle. Children learn by what they see. I was his teacher, and he was my student. Some of the lessons were good, but certainly not all of them. Early on the seeds of codependency were starting to reveal themselves in his life. Like many children living in homes with tumultuous marriages, he tried to fix Janet's and my relationship. Josh continues:

My longstanding wish was for them to work well together and love being married to each other. The emotional disconnect between them felt like a dagger in my heart. And so I did all I could to fix them. Constantly barraging them with encouragement to teach Sunday School classes **together***, to go on dates, or for us all to stay up late watching movies and have fun* **together***. My efforts never paid off, and I would get angry with my mom for pursuing lots of activities without my dad.*

That became a theme during my growing up years. I was always much harder on my mom than my dad. I would approach her about their marital issues and ask her why she was doing this or that without my dad. Looking back on it with adult eyes, I realize that I approached my mom about the subject, and was hard on her at times, because I felt safer approaching her and safer being hard on her. I never went there with my dad mainly because I thought it was my mom's fault since she was constantly out and about without him.

Once again I was "teaching." I was convinced that it was all Janet's fault. Now I was passing on that belief system to my son. Like in the shell game, "round and round she goes, where she stops nobody knows," the truth (Janet did create a life outside of me) and the lie (it's her fault) were circling around together, and where the truth lay hidden was fast becoming a mystery to Josh.

As my eyes were opened to my own issues, I had a growing sense that I had cursed my sons with the effects of "It." I was standing in church one Sunday when the weight of this realization became overwhelming. I was headed into one of those shame spirals (yes, I can still get stuck ...) when the Holy Spirit broke in and said,

I am proud of you. This has gone on for many generations, and you have broken the chain.

God was proud of me? It was unfathomable, and it ranks right up there with the most amazing thing God has ever spoken over me. Those five words would have been enough, but he also said, "You have broken the chain." How is this possible? How had I broken the chain? God has a way of speaking prophetically. He is, after all, God. Like when he called Gideon a mighty warrior when Gideon was hiding in a winepress, [53] God was stating a present truth that would reveal itself in the future. I found out later that God was already at work within Josh during the time that Janet and I were separated. Josh later wrote,

Throughout my parents' separation, I was never angry with either of them, nor did I take a side. When I was back in Texas the following summer, I stayed with my dad at my parents' house and spent plenty of time with my mom. I chose to react this way because I was finally beginning to understand that more important than them having a great marriage was their health as individuals. The circumstances broke my heart but only because I knew the pain that it caused them. Maturing into a man, I was also learning that being a son is not only about receiving love from my parents, but it is also about showing them unconditional love and support.

When I first read that paragraph from Josh a huge smile spread across my face. God was teaching him the lesson that the way to happiness and fulfillment was not through someone else (codependency), but it was through emotional and spiritual health as an individual. The effects of my "curse" were already starting to be reversed. God was showing Himself to be the same amazing redeemer and healer in my son as well.

I also have a role in the process of restoration. I have started to re-parent my adult children. As they are willing and able, we are working together to get the effects of "It" stopped, as God has promised. I am committed to stopping the effects of AED with this generation and for "It" not being passed on to the next. Josh has reached a point of amazing emotional wholeness and health in his own life. He concludes,

Today, looking back at all of those experiences, I am so very grateful that God is in the work of redeeming broken lives and emotional wounds. All of the self-discovery and healing that both of my parents have gone through has given me confidence that I can live as a healthy individual and pursue life with passion and without fear. My dad and I now have an awesome relationship that I cherish deeply. We share openly, spend quality time, and are both invested in each others' pursuits. It is every man's dream, and I am blessed.

My promise to my family, my friends and to me is that I will embrace self-reflection guided by God's Spirit in order to live as a healthy life-giving individual.

The lies have been unmasked. The light is shining, and the truth is truly setting us all free.

Now What?

The Road goes ever on
Down from the door where it began.
Now far ahead the road has gone,
And I must follow, if I can,
Pursuing it with eager feet,
Until it joins some larger way
Where many paths and errands meet.
And whither then? I cannot say. (55)

- J. R. R. Tolkien. *The Fellowship of the Ring.*

I have taken you on my journey. However, I doubt you picked up this book to read about me. There are far more entertaining pieces of literature available! You may be wondering how you can have a marriage that thrives, not just survives. We invite you to join us on this journey. The door is open. You have the opportunity for your own beginning. If you are already in counseling and have been using this book as a reference, good for you! You are well on your way to healing and wholeness. If not, below are a few things you can do.

- Find a Christian counselor or psychologist that understands AED. Make an appointment and go! Don't try to take this journey alone.
- Be completely up front and honest about **everything** with your counselor. You will only be wasting your money and time holding anything back. If you are ready, and I mean truly ready to get down to business, let your counselor know. You will start seeing the benefits of God working sooner.
- Concentrate on **you**. Do not let the focus shift to your marriage or your spouse for at least the first three months. The counselor may want to speak with your spouse to get that perspective. That's fine. However, do not let your sessions turn into marriage counseling. You read about the pitfalls of this approach in the *Why Traditional Marriage Counseling May Not Help* section of this book. If needed, change counselors. You will only be able to enjoy the relationship with a spouse if you are emotionally healthy and whole.
- If you are a man, use a male counselor. In all likelihood you will be drawn to a female counselor. It is a bit like an alcoholic being drawn toward a bar. Your subconscious is seeking more of a "fix" than getting fixed! Avoid it. Meet with a man.
- Find at least one friend that will take the journey with you. It needs to be someone that you can share **everything** that has happened to you in your past and everything that you have done in your present. This will take courage and vulnerability. However, the rewards will be great. Strongholds are often broken when the lie is exposed, and the lie must be spoken to someone else. Admitting it to yourself simply does not work. Shame likes to hide in secrets.

- Choose to trust God. Trust Him to lead you out of the darkness and into His light. Talk to Him. Cry out to Him. He will hear you. He will sustain you.

Conclusion

Books are funny things. They have an organic, living characteristic that is hard to understand. There is always one more chapter to be written, one more important point to be expressed. Unless you decide to finish them, they will never be finished. I have reached the point where the decision is made. It is time for the story of my journey to end and the start of your story to begin. I want to give two people the honor of concluding this journey. First, Gene will take you beyond my experience into some of the broader descriptions and implications of Arrested Emotional Development.

The way that I handled the abandonment and abuse in my life is not unique, but it is also not the only possible response. It is time for you to pull up a comfortable chair and join Janet and me in a casual conversation with Gene. We will explore some of the aspects of AED that go beyond our story.

A Conversation with Gene

Why is it that people tend not to change until they hit a crisis?

It is because we like to live in a comfort zone. And when we are in a comfort zone, we will remain there until something comes along to change it. It can still be "comfort" even when it is painful. I think, *at least I know about this pain; I know how to deal with it. And I know what I can and cannot do. And I know what to do to help deal with this pain.* So I will continue to live this way, choosing to do the same thing over and over again. Nothing changes. There might be a change when something is threatened, or because I want to get the other person off my back, or I think it will at least make things better for a while. But there really is no true change. Not until crisis happens.

When a crisis happens, now all of a sudden there is no choice. Change will take place, whether it is pleasant or unpleasant. Change must take place because the crisis must be resolved, either positively or negatively.

The "crisis" of the separation and impending divorce was the catalyst of change for me (Greg). In the midst of that event, there were a lot of emotions and dynamics coming at me. Will you boil it down to the essentials that paved the way for our relationship not to just survive but to grow and thrive?

Long before the separation, Janet had grown to the place where she realized that she could not fix you or change you. And she began to grow as a woman. She began to grow emotionally and spiritually, and she began to become mature in how she responded to you. You then, as a result of the crisis, began to look at yourself and began to discover that it really wasn't Janet. It was about what was going on with you. You needed to grow up and begin to take responsibility for yourself. You both began that growth process that would bring healing to your marriage and your relationship with each other. A new thing began, and it began in earnest. It all began with the starting place of, "I need to become healthy." Both of you began that process. And as a result of that process, you began to grow back together again. You began to trust each other, and you both reached the place where you began to take responsibility for yourselves and not try to be responsible for the other person.

How common is Arrested Emotional Development, or AED?

Very common! Based upon my experience, ninety to ninety-five percent of aggressive and passive-aggressive abusers are arrested in their development.

Greg's psychologist commented that he is seeing a great deal of Reactive Attachment Disorder (RAD). Is there any evidence for what may be causing the rise? Is it related to using daycares early on, moms working, chasing material possessions versus relationships with children, etc.?

I would say that fits. Not being emotionally available for your children is when *perceived* abandonment takes place. When mom is emotionally absent, it may contribute to a perceived feeling of abandonment, creating a profound fear of abandonment. When dad is absent, too passive or too aggressive, it forces the son to remain in an unhealthy attachment to his mother. Initially he needs the emotional attachment to his mother, but somewhere between eight and nine years old, a healthy transition needs to take place where he transfers from the mother to the father emotionally.

It seems like it is more common to have men stuck, shut down, and emotionally detached than women. Do you have any explanation for this?

Males can compartmentalize, so when abuse takes place at a young age, it is very common for them to never share a word of it. They put it in a box, seal it and never plan on opening that file. They may seemingly be successful in burying the pain, but not the effects on their life.

Is separating mom and wife as simple as it sounds?

No, because of all of the emotional trauma that has taken place over the years. Never being able to satisfy his mother leaves a man with the feeling that he will never be able to satisfy his wife either. A therapist can be very helpful in resolving this.

What are the signs that a man sees his mother and wife as one?

Typically it is a man who perceives his wife as having power to control and manipulate him. This leaves him frustrated and he emotionally fears abandonment...believing that every woman is going to do what his mother did to him. His general attitude is either passively or actively one of disrespect for women. On the one hand, Greg wanted nurturing from Janet or other women, but then he would fear that her nurturing left him looking weak and needy.

I (Greg) think there may be another dynamic here. At least in my case, I desperately wanted to please and receive the approval of Janet and other women in my life. This was one thing that I never believed that I was successful in with my mother. I don't think I as much disrespected women as I feared them. They were an enigma; they were easily pleased in some ways and impossible to please in others. My hypersensitive perceptions left me feeling like a constant failure.

Why are marriage counselors slow to identify and deal with these problems?

One reason is that the focus on domestic violence issues is new in the last fifteen years. Many counselors only know domestic violence from the perspective of an aggressive man or woman. In the past, many counselors were not trained in the underlying dynamics behind domestic violence. They were taught to focus on anger management and communication skills. This leads to a focus on the wife. The normal tendency is to encourage her to be more responsible in her relationship with her spouse. This is like saying to a rape victim, "If you hadn't been seductive in your walk and dress you would not have been attacked." It loses sight of the real perpetrator.

Another reason traditional counseling may not work is because the man does not believe that he has a problem. If he comes to counseling at all, it is only to help the counselor fix his wife. If the counselor does begin to focus on the husband, the husband will often abandon the counseling process.

Fortunately, there has been a dramatic change in the attitude and understanding of domestic violence from police departments to churches. Though there have been many changes, there is still a lot of room for education.

It seems that symptom chasing, "he said, she said" and the fight fair scenario is a waste of time and can make things worse, never taking the couple to a truly amazing marriage. What do you recommend?

The key is looking at the underlying cause that is keeping the cycle going. Where is the belief system coming from? How did it get started-what is the genesis of it? For sure, the guy has to get permission to grow up. That permission cannot come from a woman because she sounds like a mother who is trying to manipulate and control him. The truth is that he is the controller and master manipulator.

Both individuals get to take responsibility for their own emotions, actions, and choices. They need a new model of valuing their spouse, moving to a "Win Win" position. Understanding that there is no "Win" in the "Win Lose" scenario...only "Lose Lose." Forgiveness and empathy are necessary in the end. Creating mutuality, a safe environment to share openly and honestly, is critical.

Why is control so important to the person stuck in AED?

It's not a conscious thought, but, basically something along the lines of the following takes root in their subconscious: *I've been hurt, so I will use all of the skills I've learned up to this point in time to protect myself from further hurt. In order to do that, I must control things. Either I must control the other person or control the environment around me as best I can. And if I believe it is the other person's fault, then there isn't anything I need to change. I will use anger or whatever is necessary to maintain that safe distance from others.* Since the man with AED has a profound fear of abandonment, he will defend against further hurt at all cost.

Eventually, if he stays there long enough, he can reach the place where we are dealing with a dual personality, as Greg mentioned earlier, Dr. Jekyll and Mr. Hyde. His wife never knows which one she is dealing with. Is she dealing with the good guy? And if she is dealing with the good guy, when is the bad guy going to show up? And if the bad guy shows up, is the good guy ever coming back? She doesn't know. And that creates an anxiety; she is just not sure. This makes it difficult to predict the future and come up with a safe environment. How does she know what is going to happen next? It is that uncertainty which keeps the relationship off balance.

What effect does this unsafe atmosphere have on the relationship?

We don't know how to repair ruptures, and the other person is definitely not safe. Because the other person is not safe, I cannot share with them. Because I cannot share with them, they will not know what I'm thinking. And because they cannot know what I'm thinking, they will react in the way that makes sense to them. And the same thing is true for me. If I don't know what the other person is thinking, how can I know what is going on with them? So both people wind up not being able to share with each other their thoughts, ideas, hopes, dreams; instead they remain stuck, and the gulf widens between them, all because they do not feel safe enough to share. They have not created a safe environment. As a matter of fact, the environment is so scary, so dangerous, that neither one of them is willing to reach out to the other. They simply are reacting as time goes along. And then the crisis will eventually hit.

What does traditional marriage counseling leave out that needs to be addressed in a person with AED?

What about the shame? What about the fear? What about the perfectionism? The sexual issues? Where does it go from there? How do I get the road to assertiveness and to other issues? The key is to start by becoming that healthy adult and take responsibility for myself, no longer blaming the other person for how I feel or how I experience life. Taking full responsibility for how I express my emotions and how I share my life, and taking steps to make sure that it is safe for the other person to share what they think and what they feel, while creating an environment that makes it safe for them to just be, and where mistakes are not the end of the world. Though we disappoint one another, knowing that it will be okay.

Once this is done I will be able to repair the rupture, whatever that might be. But I can only do this after I have become healthy, realizing that I am responsible for me, not anybody else. I can only do that from an adult perspective as opposed to looking at it through the lens of a child's eyes. I am responsible for how I present myself to others. I am responsible for all of my emotions and how I express them. I am never responsible for the other person or their emotional responses. The other person is not responsible for my happiness, my sadness, nor my anger. I am totally responsible for me.

What is missing in pre-marital counseling that lets AED slip by unnoticed?

It takes two emotionally healthy adults to make up a healthy marriage. Instead of focusing on the marriage, the first period of pre-marital counseling should focus on the individuals. Ask, "What happened to you under the age of ten?" Address the real issues facing the individual. Have them read *Co-Dependent No More* or *Angry Men and the Women Who Love Them* or *When It's All Her Fault,* where necessary. Discuss the relationships they had with their parents and siblings. Greg had no memories of his mother, but no one ever suspected there was a problem even when Janet brought this up during counseling. Also, pre-verbal pain "can't" be described. If the pain occurred in the womb or prior to language skills, usually all they have are emotions. However, in the pain lies the way out from emotional trauma to healing and what would be called, a healthy person.

Too often, couples are going through marriage counseling learning how to fight fairly or improve their ability to communicate better with the primary goal of receiving a stamp of approval to get married. Unfortunately they are no closer to having a great marriage than when they started. Fixing symptoms never addresses the problems at the root of their pain. It may take time to deal with this pain, so pre-marital counseling may need to be inserted at the beginning of the engagement rather than the last six weeks before the wedding. The traumas under the age of ten are a more useful starting place than addressing control and communication issues. These can be dealt with later when both individuals are emotionally healthy and capable of positive change.

When I was diagnosed with AED/RAD, I was nearly fifty years old. What does it look like in a child/young adult, so it can be identified sooner?

One clue is that the child blames others for their problems. They seem incapable of taking responsibility for their actions, instead responding like a child in the four areas of anger, anger management, emotional relating and sexual relating. If you see a fourteen to sixteen year old consistently acting like a four year old, it may be a clue.

Notice if they consistently blame others and circumstances for their problems and difficulties. Do they tell their girlfriend how to act or how to dress? Do they prevent her from having conversations with other boys? Are they physically controlling-pushing or shoving when angry? Do they threaten to abandon the relationship if she doesn't shape up in some way? All of these are indicators AED may be present.

What can be done if these issues are caught early?

The key is to identify the victimization. Just because someone was victimized doesn't mean they have to stay a victim. You also need to identify the lies they believe based on the victimization.

When you talk to the child, you want to make sure you don't ask leading questions. The questions should be very general. What was said? Who said it? Where did it happen? Instead of asking, "Did your father hurt you? Did your father do such and such to you? By leading with the "why" you may end up with a yes, just because you asked the question in that way.

Can children really replace the lies with truth before puberty?

Usually a young child can't even speak of what was done to them. Statutory rape laws are in place because this allows the state to press charges where the proof is there but the witness is unable to identify, or they are trying to protect the predator. Children feel the need to protect the family; they don't want to create a problem that sends daddy to jail.

What are other possible responses of a child when faced with emotional pain beyond their ability to process?

Sometimes they use fantasy to escape reality. They find the distraction pleasant, but it is not necessarily healthy. Other times they use physical ways of finding that relief, for example cutting or other self-injurious behavior. The physical pain masks the emotional pain that they are experiencing. Also, acting out is not uncommon. Angry outbursts act as an emotional safety valve. Unfortunately, none of these coping mechanisms lead to healing, only fleeting temporary relief.

What can you tell us about second generation habits, the habits of children of men with AED?

Children are keen observers of their parents. Whatever they observe their parents doing, saying, or believing becomes children's reality. When they grow up and get married, they will bring the same rules to live by that they received from their parents.

It has been observed that all of us are affected by at least four generations of behavior that came before us. If a child was raised in an environment where his father was contemptuous toward women, a belief that women get what they deserve, that all women are unfaithful, that women will suck the life out of you, that you can never satisfy a woman, etc., it is likely that the attitudes have been passed down from father to son for generations. Though the son may not have AED, he is modeling someone with AED.

Do you have any other unexpected ways children perceive abandonment?

Sometimes when a parent leaves the family home because of divorce, the child will interpret their leaving as abandonment. Also because of emotional or physical trauma, a child can perceive everything through a lens of abandonment. For example, a parent or a child being hospitalized for an extended period of time, a child being raised by grandparents or being sent away to school, a parent that travels a lot though leaving a child in a safe home, can be perceived by a young child as abandonment.

What does AED look like in a woman?

Women typically do not suffer from AED. A woman's relational and holistic nature (women usually don't compartmentalize their lives) work in her favor. When a girl has a traumatic event, she is much more likely to talk to another person which helps her process her emotions. This doesn't mean that girls who have been traumatized do not suffer from issues later in life. If they do, like their male counterparts, they may also suffer from a deep sense of shame, but it generally manifests itself very differently in men and women.

However, in the case where the girl/woman chooses to bury the pain and not express it, like Greg did, her response and coping mechanisms may be similar to his.

Do you have any closing comments you feel would be beneficial?

Greg and Janet have shown you the steps that they have taken to experience the healing and restoration of their marriage. These steps are proven, and they can help anyone who has the courage to look at themselves, to be honest with themselves and to allow the living God to come in and help them make the changes that person is willing to make. But it does take risk. And it takes being willing to go to a place you have never been willing to go to before, choosing to look at those areas of your life that you may not be grown up in yet, being willing to allow the living God to help you in the business of continuing the growing process, and the willingness to make the effort to take responsibility for yourself.

Then you can begin to experience the joy and the incredible awesome closeness and intimacy that you have not been able to experience up to this point in your life. May God bless you and your spouse on this new journey. Hopefully a journey that brings you to that healthy relationship and that healthy marriage that you have been wanting. God Bless.

Janet's Dream

Last up is Janet. God gave Janet an experience so amazing that I think it will encourage you on your journey to wholeness. It all started with a coaching call followed by a dream.

I came to my coaching call on Friday afternoon feeling like a breakthrough was on the horizon that would affect a number of areas of my life. I remember mentioning something about myself as a little child. I also told my Business Coach that I felt like I just needed to cry and grieve something, but I did not know what that "something" was. Early Saturday morning I had a dream that went right to the heart of where I was struggling.

In my dream I realized that a two-year-old child was abandoned at a location earlier in the dream. I rushed back and heard this child screaming in absolute terror. Immediately, I awakened and asked, "Who is the child?"

For some time I visited various memories. First the child was a random child. Then each time I asked God, "Who is the child?" the answer was different. The second time the child was Greg. Later it was my twin siblings, especially when they were colicky. I remember being told, "Do not touch the babies. They just have to cry it out." I would stand over them trying to soothe them.

Further into processing this dream, I heard my mom say the same words to my siblings about me. This time I was the one in the playpen. "Do not touch the baby."

Later, I heard the scream in my mind as if it were from a memory in my childhood. I felt the memory as if it were real. I fully experienced the terror of abandonment, feeling completely alone, forgotten and unloved; the child was also me.

Then I remembered a baby crying itself to sleep the last two times I had arrived to visit at the beginning of a nap. Her mother had asked me to go get her. When I picked her up, she looked red faced, frantic and panicked.

As I remembered this baby, I asked God if parents are correct in leaving a baby to cry itself to sleep, forcing them to learn to facedown the fear of being alone. He said, "Parents do the best they can." He added, "I was there with the babies, and I was with you when you were alone. When Greg was raised by a detached mother, I was with him, too."

Then He said, "Remember the scream?"

I said, "Yes."

God answered, "Now you understand the scream that I gave on the cross. It was my first time ever experiencing the abandonment of God the Father. I did not scream out because of bearing the guilt of your sins. It was the abandonment."

He continued, "Abandonment from the one we love is pretty unbearable. But I want you to know that I am always there when someone is abandoned. If they want me, I will be there. Just know that I experienced it, too."

Finally He added, "I know what you are going through."

I sobbed through a lot of this discussion while the Lord Jesus and Greg held me until morning. I could not tell Greg what was wrong at the time. I was only able to relay the whole story from beginning to end once we got up for the day. It was truly an amazing and healing time for me. It has given me great empathy for those dealing with any form of abandonment, perceived or real.

Today at church, the subject of rest was discussed. We get to rest in whom we are and how we are made. What an appropriate conclusion to my weekend theme. Jesus has us. We can rest in Him. He will never leave us or forsake us. He is God. He is there.

Recommended Reading

Broken Children, Grown-Up Pain, **Paul Hegstrom, Ph.D.** - Paul's book goes into great detail on the causes and outworking of AED. If you are still wondering how AED affects you or a loved one, this is a good first read.

Destined to Reign, **Joseph Prince** - I recommend Joseph's book to propel you on your journey of the discovery of not only who you are in Christ, but whose you are. There may be a few pleasant surprises in store for you.

Healing the Shame That Binds You, **John Bradshaw** – John's book was instrumental in my journey to health and healing from Shame. I especially recommend the first two parts of the book, "PART I: THE PROBLEM – Spiritual Bankruptcy" and "Part II: THE SOLUTION-The Recovery and Uncovery Process."

Victims No Longer, **Mike Lew** – This book is a tough but necessary read if you are a man who was sexually abused. I do not recommend you read this book in isolation. You will want to be able to be open and honest with someone you trust as you process your deep emotions around the abuse that you experienced.

Sources

1. John 8:32.

2. 1 John 4:18.

3. 2 Timothy 1:7a.

4. Psalm 118:5.

5. **McGoldrick, Monica.** What is a Genogram? *The Multicultural Family Institute.* [Online] 2003-2008. [Cited: February 10, 2010.] http://www.multiculturalfamily.org/genograms.

6. **Hegstrom, Ph.D., Paul.** *Broken Children, Grown-Up Pain.* Second Edition. Kansas City : Beacon Hill Press, 2006. p. 30. ISBN: 978-0-8341-2251-2.

7. **Hegstrom, Paul.** *The DVP Handbook for Group Facilitators.* s.l. : Life Skills International, Inc., 1989. Modeled on the "Power and Control" wheels, Duluth Domestic Abuse Intervention Project.

8. **Stevenson, Robert Louis.** *The Strange Case of Dr. Jekyll and Mr. Hyde.* London : Longmans, Greene & Co., 1886.

9. **Kruszelnicki, Dr. Karl S.** Ostrich head in sand. *ABC Science.* [Online] November 02, 2006. [Cited: February 12, 2010.] www.abc.net.au/science/articles/2006/11/02/1777947.htm.

10. **Hegstrom, Ph.D., Paul.** *Broken Children, Grown-Up Pain.* Kansas City : Beacon Hill Press, 2006. pp. 16,17,45. ISBN: 978-0-8341-2251-2.

11. **Namka, Ed. D., Lynne.** Shame, The Disowned Part of the Self. *Angries Out.* [Online] 1997. Used with Permission, 2010. http://www.angriesout.com/teach8.htm.

12. **Mahari, A.J.** Awareness of the Core Wound of Abandonment Will Change Your Life. *BPD Info.* [Online] 1997. http://bpdinfo.borderlinepersonality.ca/index.php?id=51. Used with Permission, 2010.

13. **Prince, Joseph.** *Destined to Reign.* Tulsa : Harrison House Publishers, 2007. p. 131.

14. Romans 8:1.

15. Luke 7:47.

16. Matthew 9:22.

17. Matthew 26:28.

18. 1 John 2:12.

19. John 1:12.

20. Luke 15:11-32.

21. **Prince, Joseph.** *Destined to Reign.* Tulsa : Harrison House Publishers, 2007. p. 177.

22. Proverbs 23:7.

23. **Bradshaw, John.** *Healing the Shame That Binds You.* Second. Deerfield Beach : Health Communications, Inc., 2005. p. 161.

24. **Alcoholics Anonymous.** The 12 Steps of Alcoholics Anonymous. *Alcoholics Anonymous.* [Online] May 9, 2002. http://www.aa.org/lang/en/en_pdfs/smf-121_en.pdf.

25. **Bradshaw, John.** *Healing the Shame That Binds You.* Deerfield Beach : Health Communications, Inc., 2005. p. 161.

26. **Lew, Mike.** *Victims No Longer.* 2nd Edition. New York : Quill, 2004. pp. 73-76.

27. —. *Victims No Longer.* 2nd Edition. New York : Quill, 2004. pp. 6-7.

28. —. *Victims No Longer.* 2nd Edition. New York : Quill, 2004. p. 156.

29. ACE Study - Prevalence - Adverse Childhood Experiences. *Centers for Disease Control and Prevention.* [Online] September 2010. http://www.cdc.gov/nccdphp/ace/prevalence.htm.

30. Revelation 12:10.

31. James 4:7.

32. Mark 6:7.

33. Luke 10:17.

34. John 12:31, 16:11.

35. 2 Corinthians 10:5.

36. **Bradshaw, John.** *Healing the Shame That Binds You.* Deerfield Beach : Health Communications, Inc., 2005. p. 209.

37. —. *Healing the Shame That Binds You.* Deerfield Beach : Health Communications, Inc., 2005. p. 210.

38. John 8:32.

39. John 14:1.

40. John 14:2,3.

41. John 14:21.

42. Romans 8:1.

43. Philippians 4:8.

44. **Harper, Kate.** Going for a Win-Win Result - A Guide to Being Assertive. *Assertive-Skills.* [Online] 2006. Used with Permission, 2010. www.earthlingcommunication.com/a/assertive-skills/assertive-vs-aggressive-communication.php.

45. **Hegstrom, Paul.** *The DVP Handbook for Group Facilitators.* s.l. : Life Skills International, Inc., 1989. pp. 16E-55. Adapted from Michael Stuppy Seminars.

46. **Lubit, MD, PhD, Roy H. and al., et.** Child Abuse & Neglect, Reactive Attachment Disorder. [Online] October 2009. http://emedicine.medscape.com/article/915447-overview.

47. Psalm 139:13-16.

48. Acts 17:26, 27.

49. Ephesians 2:10.

50. **Smith, Ed.** What is Theophostic Prayer Ministry. *International Association for Theophostic Ministry.* [Online] 2010. Used with permission, Ed Smith, 2010. http://www.theophostic.com/page12414933.aspx.

51. Genesis 12:1.

52. **Hegstrom, Paul.** *The DVP Handbook for Group Facilitators.* s.l. : Life Skills International, Inc., 1989. Adapted from Basic Youth Conflicts, Bill Gothard. Focus on the Family Dr. James Dobson / DVP Learning Center.

53. Judges 6:12.

54. **Frost, Robert.** *The Poetry of Robert Frost.* New York : Henry Holt and Company, LLC, 1979. p. 64. ISBN: 978-0-8050-0502-8.

55. **Tolkien, J.R.R.** *The Fellowship of the Ring.* s.l. : Houghton Mifflin Harcourt Publishing Company, 1954, 1965. The Old Walking Song.